P9-CFO-246

PACIFIC FRESH

PACIFIC FRESH

o

Great Recipes from the West Coast

by

MARYANA VOLLSTEDT

CHRONICLE BOOKS
SAN FRANCISCO

Library of Congress Cataloging-in-Publication Data available.

Printed in the United States of America.
ISBN 0-8118-0391-0

Book design and illustration: Kurt D. Hollomon

Distributed in Canada by Raincoast Books,
8680 Cambie Street, Vancouver, B.C. V6P 6M9

10 9 8 7 6 5 4 3 2

Chronicle Books
275 Fifth Street
San Francisco, CA 94103

DEDICATION

To Reed, husband, chief tester, consultant, and computer person.

Throughout the years of my writing cookbooks, Reed has encouraged me with his support, advice, and assistance. We have had a lot of fun cooking together, researching new ideas, and testing recipes on family and friends. This book turned out to be a joint venture because without his countless hours and enduring patience on the computer, it could never have been accomplished.

ACKNOWLEDGMENTS

To Bill LeBlond, senior editor at Chronicle Books, for his faith in me to produce another popular and practical cookbook.

To Sharon Silva, for her expert copyediting and helpful suggestions for this book.

To friends and family, who helped critique my recipes and who would willingly come on the spur of the moment for a casual testing dinner.

TABLE OF
CONTENTS

o

INTRODUCTION
1

—

INTRODUCTORY OFFER

Hors d'oeuvres and appetizers designed to stimulate the appetite, from simple snacks to elegant first courses.

5

—

SOUP OF THE DAY

Satisfying soups for all occasions, from the hearty to the light and refreshing.

31

—

THE SALAD BOWL

A potpourri of great salads, featuring adventuresome combinations of mixed greens, garden-ripe vegetables, fresh seafood, and seasonal fruits.

51

—

CHICKEN AND COMPANY

Updated versions of some of your favorite recipes for chicken, turkey, and game hens, plus new, creative, easy-to-make oven dishes.

99

—

CATCH OF THE DAY

A selection of Pacific fresh fish and shellfish recipes that call for a variety of cooking methods and include flavorful toppings and garnishes.

125

INTRODUCTION

o

The abundance of fresh ingredients available on the West Coast makes cooking fun and exciting. Supermarkets supply us with an array of fresh fruits and vegetables the year around. Seasonal produce, picked at the peak of ripeness, can be purchased at farmer's markets and roadside stands. Quality meats and poultry are produced locally and are available at reasonable prices. Fresh fish, the variety depending upon the season, are delivered daily to markets. Cheese factories and dairies furnish us with a wide assortment of delicious and healthful dairy products. Wholesome grains, nuts, and legumes are grown and harvested in profusion. And, of course, there is the grape industry, producing internationally recognized wines in California, Oregon, Washington, and Idaho. It is no wonder the West Coast has been called a "culinary heaven"!

This constant supply of fresh ingredients has naturally influenced the style and methods of West Coast cooks. It provides a bounty of healthful foods and encourages imagination and creativity in meal planning. Cooking is never boring on the West Coast!

The mild climate and excellent growing conditions of the Pacific Coast also define the region's cooking style and lifestyle. Grilling is done almost all year long and entertaining is often casual. Barbecues, potlucks, picnics, reunions, beach parties, tailgate parties, dinner parties—almost any excuse will bring friends together to enjoy good food and drink.

Another factor that has shaped Pacific Coast cooking has been immigration. Many of the early settlers who came to the West Coast were from all parts of the world. They brought with them their cooking customs and traditions, which were passed down through the generations. This influence, along with more recent immigration, has created an interest in ethnic cooking at home and in restaurants.

I have always believed that cooking does not have to be complicated to be good. When I was working in our family retail store and cooking for six, preparing meals became a challenge. I began writing cookbooks for busy people. They proved popular because the recipes were straightforward, fun to make, and did not require a lot of preparation time. Some of those favorite recipes have been updated and included here.

Cooking in the nineties has taken a new and different direction, with an emphasis on simpler meals, smaller portions, and wholesome foods. As a result, today's time-conscious cooks are looking for recipes that can be made with ease and served with style. In this book I have taken advantage of the wealth of fresh ingredients and have included them in exciting recipes that follow the trends of the day. Enjoy with me the experience of Pacific Fresh and capture the spirit and flavor of West Coast cooking.

INTRODUCTORY OFFER

○

Here are recipes for appetizers, hors d'oeuvres, and various finger foods that can precede a dinner or form the whole menu for a wine or cocktail party. Appetizers should tease the appetite and complement the main course. Hors d'oeuvres that accompany drinks at an open house or other parties encourage a festive, friendly atmosphere.

Parties where hors d'oeuvres are served are especially popular on the West Coast during the holiday season, but they can be held anytime. Generally, they include a large assortment of contrasting foods and ingredients, both hot and cold, for guests to nibble on while socializing. We like to have our house party in the spring when over two thousand daffodils are in bloom on the five acres that surround our home. The first burst of spring and the gathering of friends puts everyone in a happy mood to welcome the forthcoming season.

Included in this section are hors d'oeuvres and appetizers that can be mixed or matched for any occasion.

BRUSCHETTA
o

Bruschetta is a traditional Italian snack of grilled bread topped with cheese, meats, anchovies, or simply a drizzle of olive oil and garlic. This topping incorporates tomatoes, cucumber, onion, and seasonings and is served as a wonderful appetizer.

3–4 tomatoes, seeded, chopped, and drained

1 cucumber, peeled, seeded, and cut into ¼-inch dice

½ red onion, cut into ¼-inch dice

½ cup lightly packed fresh basil leaves, chopped

1 clove garlic, minced

2 tablespoons olive oil

2 tablespoons red wine vinegar

Salt and pepper to taste

25 Crostini (recipe follows)

1- In a bowl stir together all ingredients except Crostini. Let stand, covered, at room temperature for several hours, stirring occasionally.

2- Using a slotted spoon, top each slice of Crostini with about 1 tablespoon of vegetable mixture. Serve immediately.

MAKES ABOUT *25* SERVINGS.

CROSTINI
○

These toasted bread slices serve as the bases for a variety of appetizers. They may be made ahead and stored for several days wrapped in aluminum foil. Serve warm or at room temperature. Make garlic oil in advance.

    ¼ cup olive oil
    2 cloves garlic, halved
    1 large baguette, cut into slices ¼ to ⅓ inch thick

1- In a small jar combine oil and garlic. Let stand several hours or overnight.

2- Preheat broiler. Arrange bread slices on baking sheet and broil on first side until lightly browned, about 1 minute. Turn slices over and brush with garlic oil. Broil about 1 minute longer.

MAKES 35 TO 40 SLICES.

Note: The bread slices may be baked instead of broiled. Arrange bread slices on baking sheet and place in a preheated 350°F oven. Bake 5 minutes, turn and brush with garlic oil. Bake until lightly browned, about 5 minutes longer.

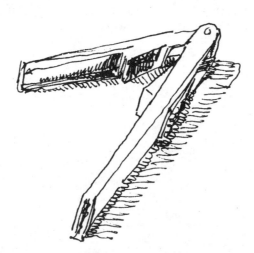

ROASTED RED PEPPER CROSTINI
o

*A colorful prelude to any dinner party. Roasting peppers results in a
wonderful smoky flavor. If you are short of time, purchase roasted
peppers in a jar.*

2 large red bell peppers

3 tablespoons olive oil

1 tablespoon red wine vinegar

2 cloves garlic, halved

¼ teaspoon salt

1½ cups grated mozzarella cheese

25 Crostini (page 7)

1- Preheat broiler. Cut peppers in half lengthwise and remove
stems, seeds, and ribs. Place skin side up on a foil-lined baking
sheet with a rim. Broil 4 inches from heat, turning to expose all
sides of the skin, until evenly charred and blackened, 10 to 15 minutes. Transfer peppers to a paper bag and close the top. Let stand
15 to 20 minutes. Remove peppers from bag and peel off skin.
Cut peppers lengthwise into strips ¼ to ½ inch wide, then cut
strips into fourths crosswise.

2- In a shallow bowl stir together oil, vinegar, garlic, and salt. Add
peppers, turn to coat, cover, and marinate 4 to 5 hours or overnight
in refrigerator.

3- Just before serving preheat broiler. Remove garlic and discard.
Arrange Crostini on baking sheet and place a spoonful of the pepper mixture on top of each. Sprinkle with cheese and broil until
cheese melts, 20 to 30 seconds. Serve immediately.

MAKES *25* SERVINGS.

CHOPPED OLIVE CROSTINI
o

If you like olives, you'll like this appetizer.

2 cans (4¼ ounces each) chopped ripe olives, drained

2 tablespoons olive oil

2 tablespoons finely chopped walnuts or pine nuts

2 large cloves garlic, minced

25 Crostini (page 7)

1 jar (2 ounces) sliced pimientos, drained

1- In a small bowl stir together olives, oil, nuts, and garlic. Spread a spoonful of mixture on warm Crostini. Top each with 1 or 2 slices of pimiento. Serve immediately.

MAKES **25** SERVINGS.

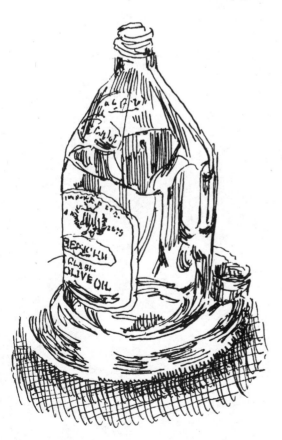

BRANDIED BRIE
o

Brie is a soft cheese with a tangy, fruity flavor and an edible rind. It can be served warm or at room temperature as an hors d'oeuvre or as a dessert cheese. Here it is dressed up with brandy and nuts. Serve the warm cheese on bagel chips, baguette slices, or any thin crackers. This preparation also makes a delightful dessert served with fresh pear and apple slices and a glass of port.

1 wedge Brie, 8 to 10 ounces

3 tablespoons brandy

1 tablespoon firmly packed brown sugar

¼ cup chopped walnuts

1- Preheat oven to 350°F. Place Brie in a small baking dish. Pour brandy over Brie, then spread sugar evenly on top. Cover with walnuts.

2- Bake until soft and warm, 8 to 10 minutes. Serve immediately with a knife alongside for spreading.

SERVES ABOUT *8*.

BAKED BRIE IN FRENCH BREAD
o

Crunchy warm garlic bread filled with melted, pungent Brie makes a mouthwatering appetizer. Also good served with soup for a hearty lunch.

1 small round loaf French bread,
   6 to 8 inches in diameter

3 tablespoons olive oil

3 cloves garlic, minced

½ pound Brie, cut up

1- Preheat oven to 350°F. Cut a round slice 4 to 6 inches in diameter from top of bread. Cut vertically at 1½-inch intervals around sides of loaf, almost to the bottom but not clear through. Remove some of the center of the loaf, leaving a 1-inch shell. Save removed bread for another use such as bread crumbs.

2- In a small bowl stir together oil and garlic. Brush inside and outside of bread with garlic-oil mixture. Fill hollowed-out bread with Brie chunks and place on baking sheet. Bake until cheese is soft but not completely melted, 10 to 12 minutes.

3- Transfer to a plate and serve immediately. To eat, pull off cheese-coated pieces from sides of bread. Cut through bottom of loaf for easier serving once sides are gone.

SERVES 6 TO 8.

Note: Bread top can be cut into strips, brushed with oil, and baked alongside loaf to be used for additional dipping.

FESTIVE GUACAMOLE DIP

○

Use the plentiful California avocado to make this dip of layers of olives, cheeses, onions, and tomatoes atop spicy guacamole. Serve with large tortilla chips for dipping into all the layers.

4 or 5 large ripe avocados, peeled and pitted

Juice of 1 lemon

1 teaspoon salt

1 clove garlic, cut up

¼ teaspoon cayenne pepper

2 drops Tabasco sauce

1 tablespoon Worcestershire sauce

1 can (4¼ ounces) chopped ripe olives, drained

1 cup grated Monterey Jack cheese

1 small red onion, chopped

2 tomatoes, seeded and diced

1 cup grated Cheddar cheese

1- Combine avocados, lemon juice, salt, garlic, cayenne pepper, and Tabasco and Worcestershire sauces in food processor. Blend to desired consistency—chunky or smooth.

2- Spread avocado mixture on a deep 10-inch pie plate. Layer on top, in order given: olives, Monterey Jack cheese, onion, tomatoes, and Cheddar cheese. Cover and refrigerate several hours until serving time.

SERVES *8* TO *10*.

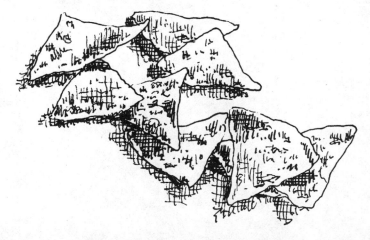

OREGON CHEESE BALL
o

It is best to assemble this mellow blend of cheeses several days in advance to allow time for the flavors to develop. The balls make terrific party fare when served with assorted crackers. Or wrap the balls in colored cellophane, attach copies of the recipe, and give as a hostess or Christmas gift.

8 ounces cream cheese, at room temperature,
   cut into pieces

¼ pound sharp Cheddar cheese,
   cut into small pieces

1 ounce blue cheese, crumbled

¼ cup mayonnaise

1 green onion, including some tender
   green tops, cut up

1 clove garlic, cut up

1 teaspoon Worcestershire sauce

1 teaspoon prepared horseradish

½ cup chopped hazelnuts or walnuts

¼ cup chopped fresh parsley

1- Combine all ingredients except nuts and parsley in food processor. Process until blended. Remove from processor and divide mixture onto 2 pieces of waxed paper (mixture will be sticky). Wrap lightly and refrigerate until easy to handle, about 1 hour. Remove from refrigerator and form into 2 balls.

2- Spread out nuts and parsley on separate plates. Roll each cheese ball first in nuts and then in parsley, to coat completely. Wrap balls in plastic wrap and refrigerate. Bring to room temperature before serving.

MAKES *2* 3-INCH CHEESE BALLS

BLUE CHEESE DIP
o

For variety, team this dip with Roasted Red Pepper and Cream Cheese Dip. Serve with raw vegetable strips and apple slices for dipping.

2 ounces blue cheese, crumbled

4 ounces light cream cheese, at room temperature, cut up

2 tablespoons mayonnaise

1 teaspoon white wine vinegar

1 teaspoon Worcestershire sauce

2 drops Tabasco sauce

1 tablespoon milk

⅓ cup chopped walnuts

1- Combine all ingredients except nuts in food processor or blender. Process until well mixed. Transfer to a small bowl, cover, and refrigerate several hours.

2- Just before serving sprinkle with nuts.

MAKES ABOUT *3/4* CUP.

ROASTED RED PEPPER
AND CREAM CHEESE DIP
○

Hors d'oeuvres should be kept simple if served before a large dinner. Offer this light dip with an assortment of fresh vegetables for dipping and munching. Carrots, jicama, cucumbers, celery, turnips, radishes, and snow peas are good choices. Leave the snow peas and radishes whole and cut the remaining vegetables into strips for serving. If possible, make the dip a day ahead to allow the flavors to develop.

    1 large red bell pepper

    2 cloves garlic, cut up

    3 ounces cream cheese, at room temperature

    ¼ cup plain nonfat yogurt or sour cream

    ¼ teaspoon dried oregano, crumbled

    ¼ teaspoon dried basil, crumbled

    ¼ teaspoon paprika

    ¼ teaspoon salt

    2 drops Tabasco sauce

1- Preheat broiler. Cut pepper in half lengthwise and remove stem, seeds, and ribs. Place skin side up in a pie plate. Broil 4 inches from heat, turning to expose all sides of the skin, until evenly charred and blackened, 10 to 15 minutes. Transfer pepper to a paper bag and close the top. Let stand until cool, 10 to 15 minutes. Remove pepper from bag and peel off skin. Cut pepper into large pieces.

2- Place pepper pieces and all remaining ingredients in food processor or blender. Process until smooth. Transfer to a small bowl, cover, and refrigerate. Serve chilled.

MAKES ABOUT *1* CUP.

SALSA MUSHROOMS
○

Serve these tasty mushrooms as an introduction to a Mexican dinner.

12 large fresh white mushrooms
Vegetable oil
½ cup Fresh Tomato Salsa (page 235) or prepared salsa
½ cup crushed tortilla chips
½ cup grated Monterey Jack cheese

1- Preheat oven to 350°F. Twist mushroom stems to free from caps and discard or save for another use. Rub both sides of mushroom caps with oil. Place mushrooms, hollow side up, in single layer in an oiled baking dish.

2- In a small bowl stir together salsa and chips. Fill caps with mixture and sprinkle with cheese. Bake until mushrooms are warm and cheese is melted, 12 to 15 minutes. Serve immediately.

MAKES *12* SERVINGS.

PUB POTATO SKINS
WITH SOUR CREAM AND BACON
o

Set the tone for a fun evening by serving crisp, baked potato skins filled with sour cream and crumbled bacon. These make good snacks with drinks, but you can also make a meal of them!

8 large baking potatoes

¼ cup butter or margarine, melted

1 cup light sour cream

½ pound bacon, fried until crisp, then crumbled

½ cup chopped green onion, including some
    tender green tops

Salt and pepper to taste

2 tablespoons minced fresh chives

1- Preheat oven to 400°F. Scrub potatoes and prick in several places with sharp tines of a fork. Bake until soft, 50 to 60 minutes. Remove potatoes from oven and let cool until they can be handled. Raise oven temperature to 425°F.

2- Cut each potato in half lengthwise. Scoop out pulp from each half (reserve for another use), leaving shell ⅛ to ¼ inch thick. Halve shells lengthwise and brush both sides with melted butter. Place on a baking sheet in a single layer. Bake until crispy, about 12 minutes. Turn potato skins over and bake until edges are crisp, about 10 minutes longer.

3- Meanwhile, in a bowl stir together sour cream, bacon, and green onion. Season pulp side of skins with salt and pepper and then top with spoonful of sour cream mixture. Garnish with chives and serve immediately.

MAKES *32* SERVINGS.

COUNTRY PÂTÉ
○

Even if you don't like liver, you'll like this pâté. The combination of meats and seasonings is so mellow, the liver is not detectable. Make the pâté at least a day in advance to allow flavors to blend and for easy slicing. Serve with baguette slices.

⅓ pound chicken livers

2 tablespoons butter or margarine

1 cup finely chopped yellow onion

1 pound ground veal

1 pound ground pork

½ cup dried bread crumbs

1 egg

½ teaspoon dried thyme, crumbled

¼ teaspoon ground allspice

¼ teaspoon Beau Monde seasoning

1 teaspoon salt

3 cloves garlic, minced

¼ cup brandy

8 slices lean bacon

Dijon Mayonnaise (page 73)

1- Preheat oven to 325°F.

2- In a small pan over medium heat, combine livers with water to cover. Bring to simmer and cook 2 or 3 minutes, then drain well and finely chop. Place in a bowl.

3- Melt butter in a small skillet over medium heat. Add onion and sauté until slightly soft, about 5 minutes. Transfer to bowl with livers and add all remaining ingredients except, bacon, and Dijon Sauce and mix well.

4- Line the bottom and sides of a 9-by-5-by-3-inch loaf pan with 5 of the bacon slices, laying them crosswise in pan. Spoon meat mixture into bacon-lined pan and pat down firmly. Place remaining 3 bacon slices on top, laying them lengthwise. Cover with aluminum foil.

5- Bake 45 minutes. Remove foil and bake until pâté is cooked through and set, 30 minutes longer. Remove from oven and pour off fat. Let cool completely. Run a knife blade around edges of pan to loosen pâté, then invert onto plate. Wrap in foil and refrigerate at least 8 hours or preferably overnight before serving. Serve with Dijon Sauce.

MAKES **20** SLICES.

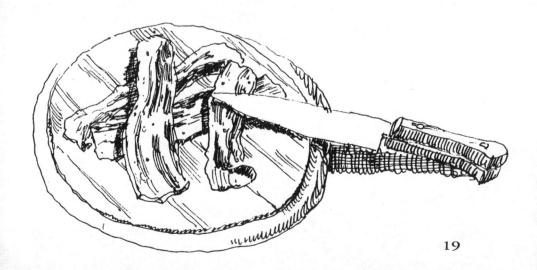

TERIYAKI WINGS
o

These tasty chicken wings make a good choice for your next cocktail party. Provide napkins—the wings are sticky. The sauce can also be used on chicken pieces for grilling.

15 chicken wings, about 3 pounds

TERIYAKI SAUCE:

½ cup soy sauce

¼ cup dry white wine

1 tablespoon vegetable oil

1 tablespoon fresh lemon juice

1 teaspoon grated lemon zest

1 tablespoon honey

2 cloves garlic, minced

1 teaspoon grated fresh ginger, or
   ¼ teaspoon ground ginger

¼ teaspoon dry mustard

1- Cut off chicken wing tips and discard or save for making stock. Separate each wing at the joint into 2 pieces and trim off excess skin. Place in a glass baking dish.

2- In a small bowl combine all sauce ingredients, stir well, and pour evenly over chicken. Cover, refrigerate, and marinate, turning once, at least 4 hours or overnight.

3- Preheat oven to 375°F. Remove wings from marinade, reserving marinade, and arrange on a foil-lined baking sheet. Bake 20 minutes. Turn wings and brush with remaining marinade. Bake until tender and browned, about 10 minutes longer.

4- Serve warm or at room temperature.

MAKES *30* SERVINGS.

SHRIMP OR CRAB DIP
○

A popular dip streamlined with lighter ingredients to reduce the calories. Serve with crackers or cocktail toast rounds.

 1 tablespoon fresh lemon juice

 8 ounces light cream cheese, at room temperature,
  cut into pieces

 2 tablespoons milk

 ¼ cup light mayonnaise

 2 fresh parsley sprigs, cut up

 ½ teaspoon dried dill

 2 drops Tabasco sauce

 Dash of salt

 1 cup chopped cooked shrimp or flaked cooked
  Dungeness crab meat

1- Place all ingredients except shrimp or crab in food processor or blender and process until smooth. Place in a bowl and fold in shrimp or crab. Cover and refrigerate several hours before serving.

MAKES *2 1/2* CUPS.

MARINATED MUSHROOMS WITH FRESH HERBS

○

Cooking the mushrooms brings out their distinctive flavor and preserves them for several days. Serve with toothpicks as an hors d'oeuvre or in a composed salad.

½ cup vegetable oil

½ cup water

Juice of 1 lemon

2 cloves garlic, cut in half

6 peppercorns

4 fresh basil leaves

2 fresh rosemary sprigs, each about
   3 inches long

6 fresh oregano leaves

2 fresh parsley sprigs

1 teaspoon salt

1 pound small fresh white mushrooms, stemmed

1- In a saucepan combine all ingredients except mushrooms. Bring to a boil and boil for 10 minutes.

2- Strain through fine-mesh sieve and return liquid to pan. Add mushrooms, cover, and cook over medium-low heat 5 minutes. Transfer mushrooms and liquid to a bowl, cover, and refrigerate several hours before serving. Drain just before serving.

MAKES ABOUT *24* SERVINGS.

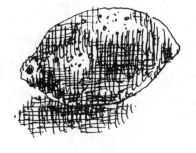

CHILLED SHRIMP

○

¼ cup water

1 cup beer, allowed to go flat

½ teaspoon salt

1 pound large shrimp, peeled with tails intact
   and deveined

Red Sauce and/or Herb-Mayonnaise Sauce
   (recipes follow)

1- In a saucepan bring water, beer, and salt to a boil. Add shrimp and cook until they turn pink, 2 to 3 minutes. Drain and place shrimp in a bowl, cover, and refrigerate several hours before serving. Offer sauces at table for dipping.

MAKES ABOUT *24* SERVINGS.

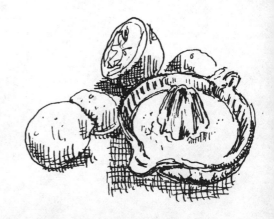

RED SAUCE
○

¾ cup catsup

¼ cup bottled chili sauce

1 tablespoon prepared horseradish

¼ teaspoon cayenne pepper

1 teaspoon fresh lemon juice

1 teaspoon Worcestershire sauce

1- In a small bowl combine all ingredients. Stir to mix well. Cover and refrigerate several hours to blend flavors before serving.

MAKES ABOUT *1* CUP.

HERB-MAYONNAISE SAUCE
○

1 cup mayonnaise

4 fresh parsley sprigs, cut up

1 clove garlic, cut up

1 tablespoon chopped fresh thyme, or
   ¾ teaspoon dried thyme, crumbled

2 teaspoons snipped fresh dill, or
   ½ teaspoon dried dill, crumbled

¼ teaspoon salt

1 tablespoon white wine vinegar

1- In food processor or blender, combine all ingredients. Process until smooth. Remove to a small bowl, cover, and refrigerate several hours to blend flavors before serving.

MAKES ABOUT *1* CUP.

CAPONATA

○

This is a wonderful and hearty hors d'oeuvre to spread on warm baguette slices. It is also good combined with pasta or served as a sauce with meats.

½ cup vegetable oil, plus 1 to 2 tablespoons
  vegetable oil, if needed

1 large eggplant, unpeeled, cut into
  1-inch cubes

1 cup chopped yellow onion

½ cup chopped green bell pepper

½ cup diced celery

3 cloves garlic, minced

1 can (28 ounces) Italian-style tomatoes with basil,
  coarsely chopped, with juices

¼ cup red wine vinegar

½ cup pitted black olives

1 tablespoon capers, drained

2 teaspoons dried oregano, crumbled

2 tablespoons chopped fresh basil leaves, or
  1 teaspoon dried basil, crumbled

1 teaspoon salt

¼ teaspoon freshly ground pepper

¼ cup toasted pine nuts (see note)

2 baguettes, sliced, buttered, sprinkled with
  Parmesan cheese, and then warmed in oven

1- In a large saucepan over medium heat, warm ½ cup oil. Add eggplant and sauté, stirring frequently, until golden brown, about 5 minutes. Remove from pan with slotted spoon and set aside.

2- Add 1 to 2 tablespoons oil to pan, if needed. Add onion, bell pepper, celery, and garlic and sauté until soft, about 5 minutes. Stir in tomatoes and juice, vinegar, olives, capers, and seasonings. Return eggplant to pan and simmer uncovered, stirring occasionally until mixture is thick and juice is almost gone, 1½ hours to 1¾ hours.

3- Stir in pine nuts and let cool. Transfer to a bowl, cover, and store in refrigerator. Bring to room temperature before serving. Top baguette slices with a spoonful of Caponata.

MAKES ABOUT *4* CUPS.

Note: To toast pine nuts preheat oven to 350°F. Spread nuts on a baking sheet and bake until golden brown, 3 to 4 minutes. Watch carefully as they burn easily.

CURRIED SHRIMP SPREAD
○

Mix this spicy spread of shrimp, cream cheese, and curry several hours in advance to allow the flavors to blend. Serve with assorted raw vegetables and crackers.

8 ounces cream cheese, at room temperature

⅓ cup mayonnaise

½ teaspoon curry powder

6 green onions with some tender green tops, chopped

¼ pound small cooked shrimp, chopped

1 hard-cooked egg, grated

1- In a serving bowl combine all ingredients except egg. Stir to mix well. Sprinkle egg on top. Cover and refrigerate several hours before serving.

MAKES ABOUT *2* CUPS.

FRESH HERB DIP

○

Fresh herbs from the garden highlight this dip. Serve with a selection of crudités or with toast rounds.

8 ounces light cream cheese, at room temperature, cut up

1 tablespoon fresh lemon juice

1 to 2 tablespoons nonfat milk

2 tablespoons light mayonnaise

2 cloves garlic, cut up

2 fresh parsley sprigs

3 fresh basil leaves, torn up

2 fresh rosemary sprigs

1 tablespoon fresh oregano leaves

1 tablespoon snipped fresh chives

10 fresh marjoram leaves

2 drops Tabasco sauce

Dash of salt

1- Combine all ingredients in food processor or blender. Process until smooth. Remove to a bowl, cover, and refrigerate several hours before serving.

MAKES ABOUT **2** CUPS.

SOUP OF THE DAY

o

Known as the "number one comfort food," a soup made from fresh ingredients is a masterpiece. What is more inviting than a pot of homemade soup simmering on the stove, filling the air with tempting aromas?

Soup making is fun and easy. I find the food processor a great aid and time-saver in slicing, chopping, and puréeing vegetables for soups. Most soups can be made in advance and reheated at serving time. In fact, they usually improve in flavor when served the next day.

Served hot or cold, before the entrée or as the main course, soups are always satisfying and bring variety to the menu. If serving soup as a first course, allow 1 to 1¼ cups per serving. If serving it as a main course, allow 1½ to 2 cups per serving. These amounts, of course, will depend on individual appetites.

The following pages are filled with an intriguing selection of hearty soups, creamy soups, garden soups, light soups, nutritious legume soups, and cold soups for all occasions.

BROCCOLI YOGURT SOUP
○

Low-fat milk and nonfat yogurt keep the calories down in this creamy soup with bright green flecks. Serve with crusty French bread or sesame crackers.

3 cups chopped broccoli florets

1 potato, peeled and sliced

2 celery stalks, sliced

1 cup chopped yellow onion

2 cups chicken broth

½ to ¾ cup low-fat milk

½ cup plain nonfat yogurt

1 tablespoon chopped fresh basil, or
   ¾ teaspoon dried basil, crumbled

½ teaspoon salt

Freshly ground pepper to taste

1 tablespoon butter or margarine (optional)

Plain nonfat yogurt, for topping (optional)

1- In a saucepan combine broccoli, potato, celery, onion, and 1 cup of the chicken broth. Cover and cook over medium-low heat until vegetables are tender, about 20 minutes.

2- Transfer to food processor or blender and purée until smooth. Return purée to pan and add remaining 1 cup broth and the milk. Using wire whisk blend in yogurt. Stir in basil, salt, pepper, and butter (if using) and heat gently to serving temperature; do not boil.

3- Ladle into serving bowls and top each serving with a dollop of yogurt, if desired. Serve immediately.

MAKES *4* CUPS.

Note: If desired, reserve 2 tablespoons chopped raw broccoli florets to sprinkle on soup when served. For a richer soup use whole milk in place of low-fat milk and sour cream in place of yogurt.

HEARTY MINESTRONE
o

When the days get cooler and appetites get bigger, it's time to make this hearty soup loaded with meat, vegetables, and pasta. It is a satisfying meal-in-a-bowl and tastes best when made the day before it is served.

¾ cup dried Great Northern or navy beans

7 cups water

1 can (16 ounces) plum tomatoes, coarsely chopped,
    with juices

1 pound cubed (1-inch cubes)
    beef stew meat

1 small yellow onion, chopped

2 carrots, sliced

1 celery stalk, sliced

1 cup shredded cabbage

1 tablespoon fresh chopped basil, or
    ¾ teaspoon dried basil, crumbled

1 tablespoon fresh chopped thyme, or
    ¾ teaspoon dried thyme, crumbled

1 bay leaf

2½ teaspoons salt

¼ teaspoon pepper

1½ cups cut-up (1-inch pieces) green beans

1 small zucchini, sliced

½ cup salad macaroni or broken
    (1-inch lengths) spaghetti

Freshly grated Parmesan cheese, for topping

1- Rinse and sort dried beans and place in a large saucepan. Add the water and bring to a boil. Boil 2 minutes. Turn off heat, cover, and let stand 1 hour.

2- Add all remaining ingredients to saucepan holding beans except green beans, zucchini, pasta, and Parmesan cheese. Bring to a simmer, cover, and simmer until beans and meat are tender, about 1 hour. Add green beans, zucchini, and pasta. Cover and simmer until vegetables are tender-crisp and pasta is al dente, about 20 minutes longer.

3- Remove bay leaf and discard. Ladle into large bowls and sprinkle with Parmesan cheese, if desired.

MAKES ABOUT **10** CUPS.

Note: For a thicker soup, purée 1 cup of the vegetables in food processor or blender. Return to soup and mix well.

POTPOURRI SOUP

○

This healthful low-cal soup is puréed, which eliminates the need for making a white sauce. You will need 6 cups mixed vegetables; carrots, celery, cabbage, and broccoli are good choices. Include in the mixture a small potato for thickening the soup and a small onion for flavor. This is one of those rainy day soups I make often because the yield is large, so the soup lasts for several days.

> 6 cups sliced mixed vegetables, including
>   1 small potato and 1 small yellow onion
> 2 cups chicken or beef broth
> 1 to 1½ cups milk
> ½ teaspoon salt
> ¼ teaspoon pepper
> ¼ teaspoon dried oregano, crumbled
> ¼ teaspoon dried basil, crumbled
> 1 tablespoon butter or margarine (optional)
> Chopped fresh parsley, for garnish

1- Combine the vegetables and broth in a saucepan. Cover and cook over medium-low heat until vegetables are tender, 15 to 20 minutes.

2- Working in batches, transfer to food processor or blender and purée. Return to pan and add milk, salt, pepper, oregano, basil, and butter (if using). Heat gently to serving temperature; do not boil. Sprinkle with parsley and serve immediately.

MAKES ABOUT *8* CUPS.

VARIATIONS:

Add 1 cup grated Cheddar or Swiss cheese with seasonings.

Add ¼ cup beer or dry white wine with seasonings.

Sprinkle each serving with freshly grated Parmesan cheese.

Omit parsley and top with crumbled cooked bacon.

CAULIFLOWER-CHEESE SOUP
◦

Cauliflower is available all year, but is served more often in winter when fewer vegetables are in season. When buying cauliflower, look for tight, creamy white flower clusters. Cauliflower is delicious raw or cooked and is especially good in this soup.

1 large head cauliflower, broken into sections
  and stalks trimmed
1 cup chopped yellow onion
2 celery stalks, sliced
1 clove garlic, cut up
1 large potato, sliced
1 cup chicken broth or water
1½ to 1¾ cups milk
1½ cups grated Cheddar cheese
¼ teaspoon dried thyme, crumbled
½ teaspoon salt
⅛ teaspoon white pepper
1 tablespoon minced fresh parsley

1- In a saucepan combine the cauliflower, onion, celery, garlic, potato, and broth or water. Cover and cook over medium-low heat until vegetables are tender, about 20 minutes.

2- Working in batches, transfer to food processor or blender and purée. Return to pan and add milk, cheese, thyme, salt, pepper, and parsley. Heat gently, stirring until cheese melts and soup is hot. Serve immediately.

MAKES ABOUT **5** CUPS.

RED PEPPER SOUP
○

Serve this colorful soup in mugs on the deck before a sunset barbecue. It can be served hot or cold. If serving cold, stir in buttermilk but do not heat. Cover and chill well before serving.

2 tablespoons vegetable oil

3 large red bell peppers, seeded and chopped

1 large yellow onion, chopped

2 cloves garlic, minced

1 small potato, chopped

½ teaspoon salt

¼ teaspoon dried thyme, crumbled

⅛ teaspoon red pepper flakes

2½ cups chicken broth

1 cup buttermilk

2 tablespoons minced fresh chives, for garnish

1- In a large saucepan over medium-low heat, warm oil. Add bell peppers and onion and sauté until tender, about 5 minutes. Add garlic and cook 30 seconds longer. Add potato, salt, thyme, red pepper flakes, and chicken broth. Bring to a boil, reduce heat, cover, and simmer until flavors are blended, about 25 minutes.

2- Working in batches, transfer to food processor or blender and purée. Return to pan and add buttermilk. Heat gently to serving temperature; do not boil. Sprinkle with chives and serve immediately.

MAKES ABOUT **4** CUPS.

WEST COAST ONION SOUP
o

Long, slow cooking of onions in butter brings out their natural sweet flavor. The addition of rich beef broth and a topping of cheese toasts turn the onions into this delicious variation on French onion soup.

¼ cup butter or margarine

4 yellow onions, about 2 pounds, thinly sliced

2 cloves garlic, minced

6 cups rich beef broth, preferably homemade

1 teaspoon Worcestershire sauce

⅓ cup dry white wine

½ teaspoon salt

¼ teaspoon dried thyme, crumbled

¼ teaspoon pepper

1 teaspoon Dijon mustard

4 slices French bread, toasted

½ cup grated Gruyère cheese

2 tablespoons freshly grated Parmesan cheese

1- In a saucepan over low heat, melt butter. Add onions and garlic, stir well, cover, and cook, stirring occasionally, until onions are limp and slightly colored, 30 to 40 minutes. Add broth, Worcestershire sauce, wine, salt, thyme, pepper, and mustard. Simmer, uncovered, until flavors are blended, abut 15 minutes. Meanwhile, preheat broiler. Pour soup into 4 individual flameproof bowls. Float slice of toast on each bowl and top toasts evenly with cheeses. Broil until cheeses melt, just a few minutes. Serve immediately.

MAKES ABOUT **7** CUPS.

Note: To help reduce the tears, chill onions in refrigerator for several hours before slicing.

ZUCCHINI-TOMATO SOUP
○

A lively summer soup of garden fresh vegetables and buttermilk with a tart flavor and creamy texture.

> 1 yellow onion, chopped
>
> 2 cloves garlic, minced
>
> 2 zucchini, chopped
>
> 1 potato, sliced
>
> 2 cups chicken broth
>
> 1 large tomato, seeded and chopped
>
> 1 to 1½ cups buttermilk
>
> 1 tablespoon chopped fresh basil, or
> ¾ teaspoon dried basil, crumbled
>
> ½ teaspoon salt
>
> Freshly ground pepper to taste

1- In a saucepan combine onion, garlic, zucchini, potato, and 1½ cups of the broth. Bring to a boil, cover, reduce heat to low, and simmer about 15 minutes. Add tomato and simmer until vegetables are tender, about 5 minutes longer.

2- Working in batches, transfer to food processor or blender and purée. Return to pan and add remaining ½ cup broth, buttermilk, basil, salt, and pepper. Simmer several minutes to blend flavors; do not boil. Serve immediately.

MAKES ABOUT *4* CUPS.

COBURG INN BEER CHEESE SOUP
○

A soup specialty from an old inn in Coburg, Oregon. The inn is no longer in operation, but this soup is still famous in the Willamette Valley and has become a favorite in many homes.

½ cup butter or margarine
½ cup diced celery
½ cup diced carrot
1 cup diced yellow onion
½ cup all-purpose flour
½ teaspoon dry mustard
5 cups chicken broth
3 tablespoons freshly grated Parmesan cheese
2 cups firmly packed grated Cheddar cheese
1 bottle (12 ounces) beer, allowed to go flat
½ teaspoon salt
Freshly ground pepper to taste

1- In a large saucepan over medium heat, melt butter. Add celery, carrot, and onion and sauté until soft, about 10 minutes. Add flour and mustard and cook, stirring constantly, 1 minute. Slowly stir in broth. Bring to a boil and cook over medium-high heat, stirring constantly, until thickened, about 5 minutes. Reduce heat, add cheeses, and stir until melted. Add beer and salt and simmer, uncovered, over low heat to blend flavors, about 15 minutes; stir occasionally but do not boil.

2- Season with pepper. Serve immediately.

MAKES ABOUT *8* CUPS.

Note: The soup thickens and texture improves the second day. Warm carefully over medium-low heat, as it scorches easily.

GAZPACHO
○

This well-known Spanish soup of garden vegetables is perfect on a hot summer day. It must be served icy cold.

4 ripe tomatoes, peeled, seeded, and chopped

1 small yellow onion, chopped

1 small green bell pepper, seeded and chopped

1 cucumber, peeled, seeded, and chopped

2 cloves garlic, minced

¼ cup chopped fresh parsley

4 cups tomato juice

1 tablespoon fresh lemon juice

1 teaspoon Worcestershire sauce

2 tablespoons olive oil

½ teaspoon paprika

⅛ teaspoon ground cumin

1 tablespoon red wine vinegar

2 drops Tabasco sauce

Salt and pepper to taste

Sour cream or plain yogurt, for topping

Lemon wedges, for garnish

1- Combine all ingredients except sour cream and lemon wedges in an attractive serving bowl. Stir well, cover, and chill thoroughly at least 4 hours.

2- Ladle into individual bowls and top with dollops of sour cream or yogurt. Serve with lemon wedges.

MAKES ABOUT **8** CUPS.

Note: For a thicker soup, before chilling, purée 1 cup of the soup in food processor or blender. Stir into remaining soup, cover, and chill as directed.

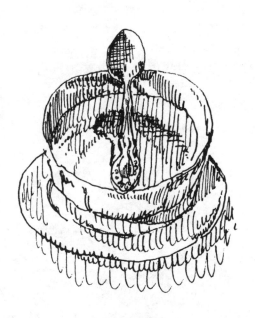

HAM-AND-POTATO CHEESE SOUP

○

A creamy, cheesy soup that is filled with ham and potato chunks. Serve with a fruit salad and warm French bread.

2 tablespoons butter or margarine
1 cup chopped yellow onion
1 cup cubed baked ham
¼ teaspoon dried thyme, crumbled
3 large potatoes, sliced
3 cups chicken broth
1 cup grated Gruyère cheese
¼ cup whole milk
Salt and freshly ground pepper to taste
Chopped fresh parsley, for garnish

1- In a saucepan over medium heat, melt butter. Add onion and sauté until tender, about 5 minutes. Stir in ham, then add thyme, potatoes, and broth. Cover and simmer until potatoes are very tender, about 20 minutes. Potatoes should be broken up and slightly mushy.

2- Add cheese and milk and stir until cheese melts and soup is heated to serving temperature. Season with salt and pepper. Keep warm over low heat, or ladle into individual bowls, garnish with parsley, and serve immediately.

MAKES ABOUT **6** CUPS.

CAPE HOUSE
OYSTER-SPINACH SOUP
○

When some fresh local oysters were brought to me during a cooking class on the Oregon coast, I came up with this recipe, combining the shellfish with chopped spinach to produce a delicious soup. Fresh oysters are available from oyster farms along the Pacific in the Northwest nearly the year around and can be purchased in the shell or freshly shucked at seafood markets and some supermarkets. This makes a great Christmas Eve soup.

¼ cup butter or margarine

1 celery stalk, sliced

1 yellow onion, chopped

1 cup chopped oysters

¼ cup all-purpose flour

3½ cups milk, or part milk and part half-and-half

1 cup chicken broth

1 cup chopped, cooked spinach, or ½ package (5 ounces) frozen chopped spinach, thawed and squeezed dry

1 teaspoon salt

¼ teaspoon dried thyme, crumbled

⅛ teaspoon white pepper

Freshly grated nutmeg, for topping (optional)

1- In a large saucepan over medium-low heat, melt butter. Add celery and sauté 1 minute. Add onion and sauté until vegetables are tender, about 4 minutes. Add oysters and cook, stirring occasionally, 2 minutes. Add flour and cook, stirring, 1 minute. Add milk and broth, bring to a boil, and stir until slightly thickened, 2 to 3 minutes. Add spinach, salt, thyme, and pepper, reduce heat to low, and simmer, stirring occasionally, until flavors are blended, about 15 minutes.

2- Ladle into individual bowls and top each with nutmeg, if desired. Serve immediately.

MAKES ABOUT **5** CUPS.

PACIFIC FRESH
SEAFOOD CHOWDER
○

Not too thick and not too thin, this chowder is a tasty blend of vegetables, seafood, and seasonings. Served with Cheese Bread, it makes a satisfying meal.

2 celery stalks, sliced

1 yellow onion, chopped

2 potatoes, peeled and cut into ½-inch cubes
  (about 2 cups)

1½ cups water

½ pound snapper or any white fish fillets,
  cut into bite-size pieces

¼ pound scallops, cut in half vertically

¼ pound small cooked shrimp

¼ cup all-purpose flour

1 bottle (8 ounces) clam juice

1½ cups light cream or milk

2 tablespoons butter or margarine

1 teaspoon salt

¼ teaspoon pepper

Chopped fresh parsley and paprika, for garnish

Cheese Bread (recipe follows)

1- In a saucepan over medium heat, combine celery, onion, potatoes and water. Cover and cook over medium heat until vegetables are slightly tender, about 10 minutes. Add seafood, re-cover and cook 10 minutes longer.

2- In a small bowl stir together flour and clam juice. Stir into fish mixture and continue to stir until bubbly. Add cream or milk, butter, salt, and pepper. Heat to serving temperature over low heat; do not boil.

3- Ladle into individual bowls and garnish with parsley and paprika. Serve immediately with Cheese Bread.

MAKES ABOUT *8* CUPS.

CHEESE BREAD
○

1 loaf sourdough French bread, halved lengthwise

Dijon mustard

1½ cups grated Cheddar cheese

1 cup grated Monterey Jack or Swiss cheese

½ cup grated mozzarella cheese

½ cup chopped fresh parsley

1- Preheat oven to 350°F. Lay bread on baking sheet and spread mustard evenly on cut sides. In a bowl and using a fork, toss together cheeses and parsley. Sprinkle cheese mixture on top of bread, then slice bread into pieces 1½ inches wide.

2- Bake until bread is warm and cheese is melted, about 10 minutes. Serve hot.

MAKES ABOUT *20* SLICES.

LENTIL, SAUSAGE, AND BROWN RICE SOUP

○

Highly nutritious lentils are the base for this hearty soup. The addition of sausage is optional, but it adds extra flavor. As with many soups, this one improves in flavor when reheated the next day.

1 cup dried lentils

½ cup long-grain brown rice

2 quarts water or chicken or beef broth,
   or a combination

2 teaspoons salt

½ teaspoon dried oregano, crumbled

¼ teaspoon dried thyme, crumbled

Freshly ground pepper

2 cloves garlic, minced

2 celery stalks, chopped

1 yellow onion, chopped

2 carrots, sliced

1 can (16 ounces) plum tomatoes,
   coarsely chopped, with juices

½ pound kielbasa sausage, cut into
   slices ¼ inch thick (optional)

1 tablespoon cider vinegar

Freshly grated Parmesan cheese, for topping

1- Rinse and sort lentils and place in a large saucepan. Add remaining ingredients except tomatoes, sausage, vinegar, and Parmesan cheese. Bring to a simmer, cover and simmer 45 minutes.

2- Add tomatoes, sausage (if using), and vinegar and simmer, uncovered, over low heat to blend flavors, 15 minutes longer. Ladle into bowls and sprinkle with cheese before serving.

MAKES ABOUT *12* CUPS.

SAUSAGE AND SAUERKRAUT SOUP

○

*My German grandfather used to make a sauerkraut soup for the family
that tasted similar to this one. At that young age I wasn't interested in
recipes, but I think he used leftover mashed potatoes. I like the cubed
potatoes better. The soup is complemented by rye bread and a glass of beer.*

2 tablespoons butter or margarine

1 pound kielbasa sausage, cut into slices ¼ inch thick

1 cup chopped yellow onion

1 large potato or 2 small potatoes, peeled and cubed
  (about 2 cups)

4 cups beef broth

½ cup dry white wine

½ teaspoon salt

¼ teaspoon pepper

1 bay leaf

1 teaspoon caraway seeds (optional)

2 cups sauerkraut, drained

1- In a saucepan over medium heat, melt butter. Add sausage and
cook, turning frequently, until well browned, about 5 minutes.
Remove with a slotted spoon to a plate.

2- Add onion to same pan and sauté until soft, about 5 minutes.
Add potatoes, broth, wine, salt, pepper, bay leaf, and caraway seeds
(if using). Cover and cook over medium-low heat 15 minutes. Add
sausage and sauerkraut and simmer, uncovered, until flavors are
blended and potatoes are soft, about 10 minutes longer.

3- Remove bay leaf and discard. Serve immediately.

MAKES ABOUT **7** CUPS.

THE SALAD BOWL

o

Salads can be served as a first course
to stimulate the appetite, alongside the main course,
after the entrée (European style), or as the centerpiece
for a luncheon or light supper.

You can be just as creative and original as you wish
when making salads. The possibilities are unlimited,
ranging from pasta salads, tossed green salads, and
refreshing fruit salads to marinated vegetable salads
and meat or seafood salads.

Tossed greens remain the country's most popular salad.
This is especially true on the West Coast, probably
because of the wealth of fresh ingredients available.
With the introduction of so-called gourmet greens,
sometimes called baby greens, mesclun, or field
greens, salads have become more exciting. Mixed
greens can be purchased in bags containing a pre-
washed assortment of mild greens (mâche, Bibb, butter, and other loose-leaf lettuces) combined with a

small amount of peppery greens (arugula, radicchio, and watercress) for a contrast in flavor, texture, and color.

Gone are the days when a green salad consisted of a wedge of lettuce and a spoonful of mayonnaise. Now salad bowls are brimming with new and interesting greens and even edible flowers.

SALAD BASICS

Select fresh ingredients. Greens must be crisp and free from bruises and brown spots. Fruits must be perfectly ripe.

—

Cover and store salad ingredients in the refrigerator in plastic bags, with the exception of mushrooms, which should be stored in a paper bag, and tomatoes, which should be stored at room temperature.

—

When making a tossed salad, allow 1 cup lightly packed torn greens per serving, plus 1 or 2 extra cups. Wash greens just before using and dry them thoroughly so dressing will not be diluted.

—

Select a dressing that complements the salad ingredients. Dressings are best if made fresh. Toss salads gently with just enough dressing to coat the ingredients lightly and then serve immediately.

—

Fruit salads are best if removed from the refrigerator ½ to 1 hour before serving.

—

When making pasta salads, cool pasta before adding dressing. Oil-based dressings can be added in advance, but creamy dressings should be added within an hour of serving time.

—

Create an attractive presentation by using interesting bowls or platters.

NORTH POINTE SALAD
○

Here is one of the few tossed salads that can be assembled in advance. Tomatoes should marinate several hours in the oil and garlic, but the dressing is added just before serving. This is one of my favorite salads.

2 tablespoons vegetable oil

1 clove garlic, minced

2 tomatoes, seeded, drained and each cut into 8 wedges

1 large head romaine lettuce

4 green onions, including some tender green tops, sliced

¼ cup freshly grated Parmesan cheese

½ pound bacon, fried until crisp, then crumbled

North Pointe Dressing (recipe follows)

1- Combine oil and garlic in a large salad bowl and mix well. Add tomatoes and stir to coat well with oil.

2- Tear lettuce into bite-size pieces and drop into bowl atop tomatoes. Scatter green onions, cheese, and bacon on top. Do not stir. Cover tightly and refrigerate up to 3 or 4 hours.

3- Just before serving, pour dressing over greens and mix salad thoroughly.

SERVES *6*.

NORTH POINTE DRESSING
○

⅓ cup vegetable oil

Juice of 1 lemon

Freshly ground pepper

½ teaspoon dried oregano, crumbled

1- In a small bowl whisk together all ingredients. Cover and refrigerate until well chilled.

MAKES ABOUT *1/2* CUP.

BASIC SPINACH SALAD
WITH VARIATIONS
o

Although this was probably the first spinach salad I ever made, I think it is still one of the best. Consider the many variations that follow.

> 1 large bunch spinach, about ¾ pound,
>   torn into bite-size pieces
> 8 slices lean bacon, fried until crisp, then crumbled
> 2 hard-cooked eggs, chopped
> 6 to 8 green onions, including some
>   tender green tops, sliced
> Basic Dressing (recipe follows)

1· In a large salad bowl combine all ingredients except dressing. Add just enough dressing to moisten thoroughly, then toss well. Serve immediately.

SERVES **4** TO **6**.

VARIATIONS:

Omit bacon and add 8 fresh mushrooms, sliced.

Omit green onions and add ¼ cup chopped red onion.

Add ¼ cup freshly grated Parmesan cheese.

Omit eggs and add ¾ cup cubed Monterey Jack cheese.

BASIC DRESSING

○

⅓ cup vegetable oil

2 tablespoons cider vinegar

1 clove garlic, minced

½ teaspoon Tabasco sauce

½ teaspoon dry mustard

½ teaspoon paprika

½ teaspoon salt

Freshly ground pepper to taste

1- Combine all ingredients in jar with tight-fitting lid. Shake well and refrigerate until chilled. Shake well before using.

MAKES ABOUT *1/2* CUP.

SPINACH-ROMAINE SALAD
WITH PINE NUTS
○

*A refreshing mix of tender spinach leaves, crisp romaine lettuce,
and pine nuts that makes a light introductory salad.*

> 1 small head romaine lettuce, torn into bite-size pieces
>
> 1 bunch fresh spinach, about ½ pound, torn into bite-size
>   pieces
>
> ¼ cup pine nuts, toasted (see note page 27)
>
> Sour Cream–Tarragon Dressing
>   (recipe follows)

1- Place lettuce, spinach, and pine nuts in a large salad bowl. Toss
greens with just enough dressing to moisten. Serve immediately.

SERVES *6* TO *8*.

VARIATIONS:

Omit pine nuts and add 1 cup sliced fresh mushrooms.

Omit pine nuts and add peanuts.

SOUR CREAM–TARRAGON DRESSING
o

1 clove garlic, minced

½ teaspoon salt

1 teaspoon fresh lemon juice

2 tablespoons tarragon vinegar, or
    2 tablespoons white wine vinegar plus
    ½ teaspoon dried tarragon, crumbled

¼ teaspoon paprika

⅛ teaspoon pepper

½ cup vegetable oil

3 tablespoons sour cream

1- In a small bowl whisk together all ingredients, except sour cream, then whisk in sour cream. Cover and refrigerate until well chilled. Whisk again before using.

MAKES ABOUT *2/3* CUP.

EAST-WEST SALAD
○

This salad highlights an interesting combination of ingredients with a Far East accent. For the greens use a combination of leaf or romaine lettuce and spinach, or whatever greens you prefer. Serve with Tandoori Chicken (page 109).

8 cups torn mixed greens

¾ cup drained, rinsed canned garbanzo beans

½ cup sliced black olives

½ small red onion, sliced

10 cherry tomatoes, halved

½ cup crumbled feta cheese, or cubed cream cheese

East-West Dressing (recipe follows)

1- Place all ingredients except dressing in a large salad bowl. Drizzle evenly with dressing and toss well. Serve immediately.

SERVES *6* TO *8*.

EAST-WEST DRESSING
○

⅓ cup olive oil

2 tablespoons white wine vinegar

1 clove garlic, minced

¼ teaspoon dry mustard

⅛ teaspoon ground cumin

½ teaspoon paprika

¼ teaspoon salt

Freshly ground pepper to taste

1- Combine all ingredients in jar with tight-fitting lid. Shake well and refrigerate until well chilled. Shake well before using.

MAKES ABOUT *1/2* CUP.

BISTRO SALAD
o

In a small restaurant in Seattle, I was served a salad similar to this one. It is a great combination of ingredients that goes well with any entrée.

½ head red-leaf lettuce, torn into bite-size pieces

½ head romaine lettuce, torn into bite-size pieces

7 or 8 fresh mushrooms, sliced

½ cup chopped red onion

2 avocados, peeled, pitted, and sliced lengthwise

3 ounces blue cheese, crumbled

½ cup walnut pieces

Bistro Dressing (recipe follows)

1- Place all ingredients except dressing in a large salad bowl. Drizzle evenly with dressing and toss well. Serve immediately.

SERVES *6*.

BISTRO DRESSING
o

½ cup vegetable oil

¼ cup red wine vinegar

1 tablespoon orange juice

4 or 5 fresh basil leaves, chopped, or
   1 teaspoon dried basil, crumbled

1 fresh parsley sprig

2 cloves garlic, halved

½ teaspoon salt

⅛ teaspoon pepper

1- Place all ingredients in food processor or blender. Process to blend well. Cover and refrigerate until ready to use.

MAKES ABOUT *3/4* CUP.

NEW CAESAR SALAD
o

Crisp romaine, freshly grated Parmesan cheese, and homemade croutons are the traditional ingredients of this popular salad. Mix in an over-sized bowl so you can toss it with flair. The no-egg dressing has just a hint of anchovy, but more can be added to suit your taste.

1 large head romaine lettuce, torn into bite-size pieces

1 cup Garlic Croutons (recipe follows)

⅓ cup freshly grated Parmesan cheese

Caesar-Style Dressing (recipe follows)

Anchovy fillets, for garnish (optional)

1- Place lettuce, croutons, and cheese in a large salad bowl. Drizzle dressing evenly over top and toss well. Garnish with anchovies. Serve immediately.

SERVES *4* TO *6*.

VARIATIONS:

Add 1 cup small cooked shrimp to salad before tossing.

Add ½ cup sliced green onion, including some tender green tops, or ¼ cup chopped red onion to salad before tossing.

Add ½ cup sliced fresh mushrooms to salad before tossing.

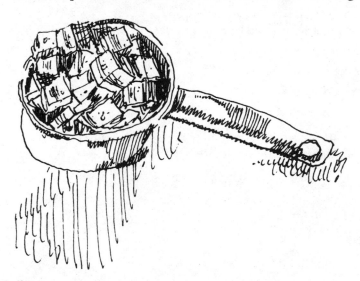

CAESAR-STYLE DRESSING
o

¼ cup olive oil

¼ cup vegetable oil

1 tablespoon freshly grated Parmesan cheese

3 tablespoons fresh lemon juice

1 green onion, including some tender green tops, cut up

2 cloves garlic, cut up

½ teaspoon dry mustard

1 to 2 teaspoons anchovy paste, or more to taste

1 teaspoon Worcestershire sauce

¼ teaspoon pepper

1- In food processor or in blender combine all ingredients. Process to blend well. Cover and refrigerate until ready to use.

MAKES ABOUT *3/4* CUP.

Note: For a stronger-flavored dressing, substitute 2 or 3 anchovy fillets for the anchovy paste.

GARLIC CROUTONS
o

2 tablespoons butter or margarine

1 tablespoon vegetable oil

2 cloves garlic, minced

2 cups cubed (1½-inch cubes) French bread

1- In a nonstick skillet over medium heat, melt butter with oil. Add garlic and sauté 1 minute. Raise temperature to medium-high and add bread cubes and toss until lightly browned, about 5 minutes. Remove from heat and let cool. Store at room temperature in an airtight container up to 1 week.

MAKES ABOUT *2* CUPS.

CALIFORNIA SALAD
○

A taste of California—juicy sweet oranges, buttery avocados, and crisp onion rings tossed with a sweet-and-sour dressing. For greens use leafy lettuce, romaine lettuce, frisée, or greens of your choice.

> 6 to 8 cups mixed torn salad greens
>
> 1 white sweet onion, thinly sliced and separated into rings
>
> 2 avocados, peeled, pitted, and sliced
>
> 2 fresh oranges, peeled, cut into bite-size pieces, and drained
>
> California Dressing (recipe follows)

1- Place greens, onion, avocados, and oranges in a large salad bowl. Drizzle evenly with dressing and toss to coat well. Serve immediately.

SERVES **6**.

CALIFORNIA DRESSING
○

> 1 tablespoon chopped yellow onion
>
> 2 tablespoons cider vinegar
>
> 2½ tablespoons sugar
>
> ½ teaspoon dry mustard
>
> ½ teaspoon salt
>
> ½ teaspoon paprika
>
> 1½ teaspoons celery seeds
>
> ½ cup vegetable oil

1- Place all ingredients except oil in food processor or blender. Process to blend well. With motor running, slowly pour in oil and continue to process until blended. Cover and refrigerate until serving time.

MAKES ABOUT **3/4** CUP.

Orange-Gorgonzola Salad with Poppy-Seed Dressing
○

The savory, sharp flavor of Gorgonzola complements the oranges and is enhanced by Poppy-Seed Dressing.

6 to 8 cups mixed torn salad greens
2 oranges, peeled, cut into bite-size pieces, and drained
6 green onions, including some tender green tops, sliced
4 ounces Gorgonzola cheese, crumbled
¼ cup toasted slivered almonds (see note)
Poppy-Seed Dressing (recipe follows)

1- Place greens, oranges, onions, cheese, and almonds in a large salad bowl. Drizzle evenly with dressing and toss to coat well. Serve immediately.

SERVES **6**.

Note: To toast almonds, preheat oven to 400°F. Spread nuts in small pan and bake, stirring once, until lightly toasted, about 8 minutes.

Poppy-Seed Dressing
○

2 tablespoons honey
½ teaspoon dry mustard
½ teaspoon paprika
2 tablespoons fresh lemon juice
1½ teaspoons white wine vinegar
½ cup vegetable oil
1½ teaspoons poppy seeds

1- Place all ingredients except oil and poppy seeds in food processor or blender. Process to blend well. With motor running, slowly pour in oil and continue to process until well blended. Remove to bowl and stir in poppy seeds. Cover and refrigerate until serving time.

MAKES ABOUT **3/4** CUP.

HAZELNUT SALAD
o

Mixed greens, sometimes identified as spring mix, are available in most markets. The combination generally includes a mix of mild greens with a few bitter greens for accent. Nut oils add an aromatic flavor to any salad. Oregon is the leading state in the country in the production of hazelnuts (also called filberts). They can be stored in an airtight container in the freezer for up to six months.

6 to 8 cups mixed torn greens

1 red onion, thinly sliced and separated into rings

¼ cup crumbled Gorgonzola cheese

¼ cup hazelnuts, toasted (see note) and coarsely chopped

Hazelnut Dressing (recipe follows)

1- Place greens, onion, cheese, and nuts in a large salad bowl. Drizzle evenly with dressing and toss to coat well. Serve immediately.

SERVES **6**.

Note: To toast hazelnuts, preheat oven to 350°F. Spread nuts on a baking sheet and bake until lightly colored and skins are blistered, 12 to 15 minutes. Wrap hot nuts in cotton towel to steam 1 minute. Then rub the nuts in the towel to remove most of the skins.

HAZELNUT DRESSING
o

3 tablespoons hazelnut oil

3 tablespoons olive oil

3 tablespoons white wine vinegar

1 teaspoon Dijon mustard

¼ teaspoon salt

⅛ teaspoon pepper

1- In a small bowl whisk together all ingredients. Cover and refrigerate until serving time.

MAKES ABOUT **1/2** CUP.

LEMON-MUSHROOM SALAD
○

A company salad of lemony mushrooms piled on a bed of tender butter lettuce leaves. This is a refreshing salad to serve after a heavy entrée.

½ pound fresh mushrooms, sliced
Lemon Dressing (recipe follows)
Butter lettuce

1- Place mushrooms in a bowl. Pour on dressing and toss lightly. Cover and refrigerate 4 to 5 hours.

2- Arrange lettuce leaves on 4 individual plates. Using slotted spoon divide mushrooms among plates. Spoon some dressing over each salad. Serve immediately.

SERVES *4*.

LEMON DRESSING
○

Juice of 1 lemon
½ cup vegetable oil
⅓ teaspoon sugar
¼ teaspoon freshly ground pepper
¼ teaspoon dried basil, crumbled
¼ teaspoon dried marjoram, crumbled
¼ teaspoon dried oregano, crumbled
⅓ teaspoon salt
⅛ teaspoon garlic powder

1- Combine all ingredients in jar with tight-fitting lid. Shake well and refrigerate until well chilled. Shake well before using.

MAKES ABOUT *3/4* CUP.

SHOWCASE SALAD
○

This colorful composed salad of vivid red beets, bright green beans, and earthy mushrooms always brings compliments. Two dressings, one oil-based, one creamy, add zest and flavor.

1 pound green beans, trimmed

1 cup Reed's Own Dressing (page 95)

½ pound fresh mushrooms, quartered

1 pound beets

6 cups water

Romaine lettuce leaves, for lining platter

Radicchio or red cabbage leaves, for lining platter

1 large red onion, sliced and separated into rings

8 to 10 cherry tomatoes, for garnish

¼ cup Horseradish Cream (page 96)

1- In a large saucepan bring enough water to cover beans to a boil. Drop beans into water and boil until tender-crisp, about 4 minutes. Drain and immerse in cold water to stop cooking. Drain again and place in a bowl. Add just enough Reed's Own Dressing to moisten beans and toss to coat evenly. Cover and marinate 7 or 8 hours or overnight in refrigerator.

2- In a bowl toss mushrooms with remaining dressing to coat evenly. Cover and marinate 7 or 8 hours or overnight in refrigerator.

3- Cut off all but 1 inch of beet tops. Wash beets but leave whole with roots attached. In a large saucepan bring the water to a boil. Add beets, cover, reduce heat to medium-low, and cook until beets are tender, 30 to 40 minutes. Drain and rinse under cold running water. Slip off skins and remove tops and roots. Slice beets, cover, and refrigerate until well chilled.

4- To assemble salad, place romaine leaves at one end of a large platter and radicchio leaves at opposite end. Arrange beans on radicchio leaves and beets on romaine leaves. Mound mushrooms in center, top with onion rings, and garnish with tomatoes. Spread Horseradish Cream on beets, but do not cover entirely. Serve at once.

SERVES *6* TO *8*.

VARIATIONS:

Add pitted black olives.

Add red or green pepper strips.

Add sliced avocado.

CHOPPED SALAD
WITH BALSAMIC VINAIGRETTE
o

Try this easy-to-make Italian-inspired salad of vegetables, meats, and cheese. It should be made several hours ahead to allow flavors to blend. Serve for a luncheon or light supper.

2 tomatoes, seeded, chopped, and drained
on paper towels for 30 minutes

1 cucumber, seeded and chopped

½ green bell pepper, seeded and chopped

6 green onions, including some tender green tops, sliced

¼ cup chopped red onion

¼ pound sliced dry salami, cut into bite-size pieces

1 cup cubed mozzarella cheese

¾ cup sliced, pitted black olives

4 to 5 cups finely shredded lettuce

Balsamic Vinaigrette (recipe follows)

1- In a bowl combine tomatoes, cucumber, bell pepper, onions, salami, cheese, and olives. Drizzle with just enough dressing to moisten, then toss gently to mix. Cover and refrigerate several hours. Stir several times.

2- To serve, divide lettuce evenly among 6 individual plates. Spoon vegetable mixture on top and serve immediately.

SERVES *6*.

BALSAMIC VINAIGRETTE
○

⅔ cup olive oil

3 tablespoons balsamic vinegar (see note) or
   red wine vinegar

1 clove garlic, minced

1 tablespoon chopped fresh basil, or
   ¼ teaspoon dried basil, crumbled

2 teaspoons fresh lemon juice

½ teaspoon sugar

½ teaspoon salt

⅛ teaspoon pepper

1- Combine all ingredients in jar with tight-fitting lid. Shake well before using.

MAKES ABOUT *1* CUP.

Note: Balsamic vinegar is a sweet aromatic vinegar produced in Italy. It adds lively flavor to salads, meats, and vegetables.

LAYERED POTATO SALAD
WITH HORSERADISH DRESSING
o

Potatoes, eggs, onions, parsley, and dressing layered in a glass bowl make this salad an appealing presentation. Make a day in advance to allow the flavors to blend. A superb salad to take to a potluck or picnic.

> 10 red new potatoes, about 3 ½ pounds,
>   unpeeled, halved lengthwise
>
> ¼ teaspoon salt, plus salt to taste
>
> 1 cup finely chopped fresh parsley
>
> 1 cup chopped green onions, including
>   some tender green tops
>
> 6 hard-cooked eggs, chopped
>
> Horseradish Dressing (recipe follows)
>
> Paprika, for sprinkling on top

1- Place potatoes in a saucepan and add cold water to cover and ¼ teaspoon salt. Cover, bring to a boil, reduce heat, and cook over medium-low heat until tender, 20 to 25 minutes. Drain well and let cool; do not peel. Slice crosswise into bite-size pieces.

2- In a small bowl stir together parsley and onions.

3- Forming layers, place one third of the sliced potatoes on bottom of a large glass bowl. Sprinkle lightly with salt. Spread on one third of dressing, then top with one third of eggs and then one third of parsley-onion mixture. Repeat layering twice, ending with parsley-onion mixture. Do not stir. Sprinkle with paprika.

4- Cover and refrigerate for 8 hours or overnight before serving.

SERVES *8* TO *10*.

HORSERADISH DRESSING
○

1½ cups light mayonnaise
½ cup light sour cream
½ cup plain nonfat yogurt
1 teaspoon celery seeds
½ teaspoon dry mustard
½ teaspoon salt
¼ teaspoon pepper
1 tablespoon prepared horseradish

1- In a bowl stir together all ingredients until well blended.

MAKES ABOUT **3** CUPS.

Note: This dressing is also good on cooked vegetables and grilled hamburgers.

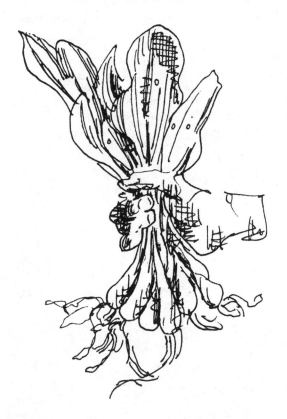

FRENCH POTATO SALAD WITH MUSTARD VINAIGRETTE

○

For a change from the traditional creamy potato salad, try this version of new potatoes mixed with a vinaigrette and topped with a spoonful of Dijon-flavored mayonnaise.

> 6 red new potatoes, about 2 pounds, unpeeled,
>   halved lengthwise
> ¼ teaspoon salt
> 6 green onions, including some tender green tops, sliced
> ¼ cup chopped fresh parsley
> Mustard Vinaigrette (recipe follows)
> Dijon Mayonnaise (recipe follows, optional)

1- Place potatoes in a saucepan and add cold water to cover and salt. Cover, bring to a boil, reduce heat, and cook over medium-low heat until tender, 20 to 25 minutes. Drain well and let cool; do not peel. Cut into bite-size pieces.

2- Place potatoes, onions, and parsley in a bowl. Add vinaigrette and toss lightly. Cover and refrigerate 6 to 8 hours.

3- To serve, spoon onto individual plates and top each portion with a spoonful of Dijon Mayonnaise, if desired.

SERVES *4* TO *6*.

MUSTARD VINAIGRETTE
❍

⅓ cup olive oil

3 tablespoons white wine vinegar

1 teaspoon fresh lemon juice

1 clove garlic, minced

1 tablespoon Dijon mustard

¼ teaspoon dried tarragon, crumbled

¼ teaspoon dried oregano, crumbled

¼ teaspoon salt

⅛ teaspoon pepper

1- In a small bowl whisk together all ingredients until well blended.

MAKES ABOUT *1/2* CUP.

DIJON MAYONNAISE
❍

¼ cup mayonnaise

¼ cup plain nonfat yogurt

1 tablespoon Dijon mustard

1 teaspoon lemon juice

1- In a small bowl stir together all ingredients until well blended. Cover and refrigerate until chilled.

MAKES ABOUT *1/2* CUP.

MARINATED TOMATOES, CUCUMBERS, AND FETA CHEESE

○

Bright red tomatoes contrast sharply with the white feta cheese, cucumbers, and black olives in this Greek-inspired salad.

1 red onion, thinly sliced and separated into rings

4 tomatoes, thickly sliced

1 cucumber, sliced

Oil and Vinegar Dressing (recipe follows)

¼ cup Greek olives

⅓ cup crumbled feta cheese

2 tablespoons chopped fresh parsley

1- Arrange onion rings, tomatoes, and cucumbers in a rimmed platter or pie plate and pour dressing evenly over top. Scatter olives over top. Cover and refrigerate several hours.

2- Just before serving sprinkle on feta cheese and parsley.

SERVES *6*.

Note: For a milder onion taste, place onion rings in a small bowl and add water to cover. Let stand 30 minutes. Drain and pat dry.

OIL AND VINEGAR DRESSING
○

½ cup vegetable oil

3 tablespoons red wine vinegar

1 clove garlic, minced

3 or 4 fresh basil leaves, chopped, or
   ½ teaspoon dried basil, crumbled

1 teaspoon chopped fresh oregano, or
   ¼ teaspoon dried oregano, crumbled

¼ teaspoon dry mustard

½ teaspoon salt

Freshly ground pepper to taste

1- In a small bowl whisk together all ingredients until blended.

MAKES ABOUT *3/4* CUP.

FARMER'S MARKET SALAD

○

A walk through Seattle's Pike Street market gave me the inspiration for this salad. Select seasonal vegetables and create your own market salad.

3 tomatoes, seeded, sliced, and drained
on paper towels for 30 minutes

8 fresh mushrooms, sliced

1 cucumber, peeled, seeded, and sliced

6 radishes, sliced

½ green bell pepper, seeded and sliced into rings

½ red onion, thinly sliced and separated into rings

Oil and Vinegar Dressing (page 75)

Salt and pepper to taste

½ cup cubed Monterey Jack cheese

2 hard-cooked eggs, quartered

¼ cup pitted whole black olives

4 anchovy fillets (optional)

1- In a large glass salad bowl arrange all sliced vegetables in layers, drizzling dressing and sprinkling salt and pepper on each layer. Cover and refrigerate several hours.

2- Add cheese, egg wedges, olives, and anchovies on top before serving. Do not toss.

SERVES *4*.

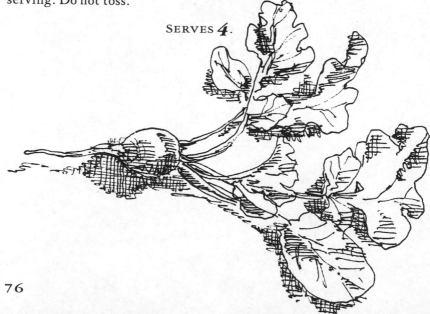

CRAZY CABBAGE

o

This salad is a perfect accompaniment to ribs and beans. It is best when eaten soon after mixing, but will keep for a few days in the refrigerator if necessary.

1 yellow onion, chopped

⅓ cup sugar

½ cup vegetable oil

½ cup cider vinegar

½ cup mayonnaise

1 teaspoon salt

1 large head green cabbage, shredded and chilled

1- In a bowl combine onion and sugar. Let stand at room temperature 30 minutes. Add oil, vinegar, mayonnaise, and salt. Whisk to blend. Cover and refrigerate.

2- Mix dressing with cabbage 1 to 2 hours before serving.

3- Mix well before serving and serve with a slotted spoon.

SERVES *8*.

CUCUMBERS WITH SOUR CREAM
○

Cucumbers are available the year around, but those fresh from the garden are the best. Serve with grilled salmon or other grilled fish.

3 cucumbers, peeled and thinly sliced

1 teaspoon salt

¼ cup chopped green onion, including some tender green tops

½ cup sour cream

1 tablespoon sugar

2 tablespoons cider vinegar

Freshly ground pepper to taste

1- Layer cucumber slices in a shallow bowl, sprinkling each layer with salt. Lay a paper towel on top of cucumbers. Top with another bowl to weight down cucumbers and let stand 1 hour at room temperature.

2- Drain cucumbers well and pat dry with paper towels. In a small bowl stir together onion, sour cream, sugar, vinegar, and pepper. Combine onion mixture with cucumbers and mix well. Cover and refrigerate several hours or overnight before serving.

SERVES *4*.

VARIATION:

Add 1 tablespoon chopped fresh dill or 1 teaspoon dried dill to the onion mixture.

SUMMERTIME PASTA SALAD
○

Pasta salads need a zesty dressing to make a statement. Use Reed's Own Dressing on this popular combination.

1 cup cherry tomatoes, halved

8 ounces (2½ cups) corkscrew pasta, fusilli, or rotini, cooked until al dente, drained, and cooled

¼ cup chopped fresh parsley

¼ cup finely chopped fresh basil

6 green onions, including some tender green tops, sliced

½ red bell pepper, seeded and diced

¼ pound sliced dry salami, cut into strips

1 cup drained, rinsed canned garbanzo beans

3–4 ounces feta cheese, cut into small dice

¼ cup freshly grated Parmesan cheese

Salt and pepper to taste

Reed's Own Dressing (page 95)

1- Place tomatoes cut side down on paper towels to drain 10 minutes.

2- In a large salad bowl place pasta. Add drained tomatoes and all remaining ingredients except dressing. Drizzle dressing evenly over top and toss to mix well.

3- Cover and refrigerate 4 hours before serving.

SERVES **6**.

PASTA SALAD WITH CHICKEN
o

A basic luncheon standby and a good way to use up leftover cooked chicken or turkey. Serve with fresh pineapple slices, cantaloupe spears, and warm croissants.

2 to 3 cups cubed, cooked chicken, preferably breast meat

½ cup chopped red bell pepper

½ cup chopped red onion

½ cup sliced celery

1 cup seedless green grapes

¼ cup slivered blanched almonds

½ cup pitted black olives

8 ounces (2½ cups) rotini or fusilli, cooked al dente, drained, and cooled

Creamy Dressing (recipe follows)

1- In a bowl combine all ingredients except dressing. Stir to mix well. Cover and refrigerate several hours.

2- Mix in dressing 1 hour before serving.

SERVES **6**.

CREAMY DRESSING
o

¾ cup mayonnaise

¼ cup plain nonfat yogurt

1 tablespoon fresh lemon juice

1 teaspoon Dijon mustard

¼ teaspoon Beau Monde seasoning

¼ teaspoon salt

⅛ teaspoon white pepper

1- In a small bowl stir together all ingredients. Cover and refrigerate.

MAKES ABOUT **1** CUP.

CHICKEN SALAD WITH PESTO MAYONNAISE

○

Here is a good summer luncheon salad of chunky chicken with a fresh pesto mayonnaise dressing. For dessert, offer a light sorbet.

2 celery stalks, sliced

½ red onion, chopped

2 cups cubed, cooked chicken

½ cup mayonnaise

2 tablespoons Basil Pesto (page 247) or
    prepared pesto (see note)

Salt and pepper to taste

Shredded lettuce

Tomato wedges, for garnish

Pitted black olives, for garnish

1- In a bowl stir together celery, onion, and chicken. In a small bowl stir together mayonnaise and pesto and add to chicken mixture. Season with salt and pepper and mix well. Cover and refrigerate until chilled.

2- To serve, line 4 individual plates with lettuce. Divide chicken mixture evenly among plates. Garnish with tomato wedges and olives.

SERVES *4*.

Note: Purchased pesto may be used. If necessary, drain off any excess oil.

LAYERED DUNGENESS CRAB SALAD

○

The famed Dungeness crab is named after a small town on the Olympic Peninsula in Washington State. It is well known as a delicacy throughout the country for its mild, sweet flavor and tender texture. This variation on a crab Louis should be made about 4 hours in advance to allow the flavors to develop.

> 1 cup shredded lettuce
>
> ½ pound cooked Dungeness crab meat, picked over for shell fragments and flaked
>
> ½ red bell pepper, seeded and diced
>
> 2 celery stalks, sliced
>
> 6 green onions, including some tender green tops, sliced
>
> 3 hard-cooked eggs, sliced
>
> Creamy Horseradish Dressing (recipe follows)

1- Place lettuce in the bottom of a glass serving bowl. Top with half the crab, bell pepper, celery, onions, and eggs, arranging ingredients in a single layer. Top with half the dressing. Repeat layer. Top with remaining dressing. Do not stir.

2- Cover and refrigerate up to 4 hours before serving.

SERVES **4**.

CREAMY HORSERADISH DRESSING
○

¾ cup mayonnaise

¼ cup nonfat plain yogurt

1 tablespoon fresh lemon juice

1 tablespoon prepared horseradish

1 tablespoon chopped fresh chives

¼ teaspoon paprika

¼ teaspoon celery salt

¼ teaspoon salt

¼ teaspoon dry mustard

1- In a small bowl stir together all ingredients. Cover and refrigerate until needed.

MAKES ABOUT *1* CUP.

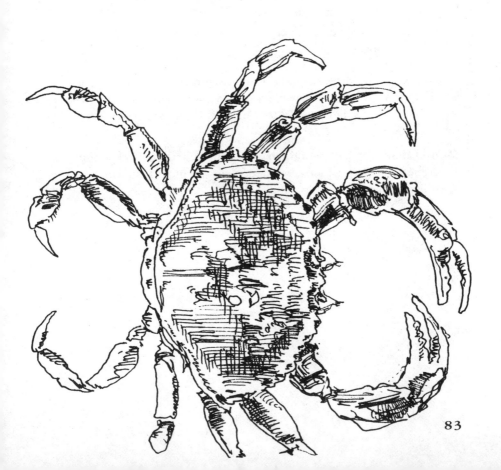

SHRIMP PASTA SALAD

○

In this salad small cooked shrimp, sometimes called bay or salad shrimp, are used. This makes a nice luncheon salad served with warm crusty bread.

8 ounces (2 ½ cups) shell pasta
   (1-inch), cooked al dente, drained, and cooled
1 red bell pepper, seeded and diced
6 green onions, including some tender green tops, sliced
2 celery stalks, sliced
2 avocados, peeled, pitted, and cut into bite-size pieces
2 tablespoons fresh lemon juice
½ pound cooked small bay shrimp
Creamy Italian Dressing (page 93)
Salt and freshly ground pepper, to taste
Lettuce leaves, for lining plates
3 hard-cooked eggs, quartered, for garnish
Salt and freshly ground pepper to taste

1- In a bowl combine pasta, bell pepper, onions, and celery and stir to mix well. In a separate bowl toss avocados with lemon juice and then add to salad along with shrimp. Cover and refrigerate several hours.

2- Add about 1 cup dressing, salt, and pepper, and mix well 1 hour before serving. Line a platter with lettuce and mound salad on top. Garnish with eggs and serve immediately.

SERVES *4* TO *6*.

PEAR SALAD WITH GORGONZOLA AND WALNUTS

o

This wonderful Italian salad combines juicy fresh pears, tangy Gorgonzola cheese, and chopped walnuts. If you like, increase the Gorgonzola and walnuts to taste.

> 1 head butter lettuce, torn into large pieces
>
> 2 ripe pears
>
> ¼ cup crumbled Gorgonzola cheese
>
> 8 teaspoons Raspberry Vinaigrette (page 96), or
>   4 teaspoons mayonnaise
>
> ¼ cup coarsely chopped walnuts

1- Line 4 individual plates with lettuce. Peel, halve, and core pears. Cut into slices ¼ inch thick. Arrange pear slices on lettuce in a circle. Sprinkle equal amount of cheese over top of each. Drizzle about 2 teaspoons Raspberry Vinaigrette over each salad, or top center of each salad with 1 teaspoon mayonnaise. Sprinkle with walnuts and serve immediately.

SERVES *4*.

VARIATION:

Just before a dinner, Reed brought home pears for this salad. They were hard, green, and tasteless and would not do. I had to come up with a last-minute substitute and since we had lots of cantaloupe on hand, I decided to try cantaloupe spears. The result was wonderful and a new recipe was developed.

FRESH FRUIT SALAD
WITH CURRY DRESSING
o

Fruit salads are so versatile, almost any fruits can be combined with good results. Alter this salad with seasonal fruits of your choice.

1 green apple, cored and chopped

2 red apples, cored and chopped

2 tablespoons fresh lemon juice

½ cup water

1 cup cubed fresh pineapple

1 cup seedless green grapes

⅓ cup chopped walnuts

¾ cup blueberries

Curry Dressing (recipe follows)

1- In a bowl combine apples, lemon juice, and water. Toss and let stand 5 minutes. Drain apples and combine with other fruits, except blueberries, in a 1½-quart glass bowl. Cover and refrigerate several hours.

2- Add blueberries and nuts to fruit mixture just before serving and toss lightly. Serve with Curry Dressing on the side.

SERVES **6** TO **8**.

Note: Sliced fresh peaches or pears are good additions.

CURRY DRESSING

○

¾ cup plain nonfat yogurt

1 tablespoon honey

1 teaspoon fresh lemon or lime juice

¼ teaspoon curry powder

Dash of ground cinnamon

1- In a small bowl stir together all ingredients. Cover and refrigerate until well chilled before using.

MAKES ABOUT *3/4* CUP.

FRUIT PLATTER WITH HONEY-YOGURT DRESSING

○

Use an assortment of summer fruits in season to make this pretty platter. Offer the tangy-sweet dressing in a bowl on the side.

Grape leaves or lettuce leaves, for lining plate

1 cantaloupe, peeled, seeded, and sliced

2 oranges, peeled and sliced

2 peaches, pitted and sliced

1 kiwi fruit, peeled and sliced

1 large bunch green grapes

1 cup strawberries or raspberries

1 avocado, peeled, pitted, and sliced

1 tablespoon fresh lemon juice

Honey-Yogurt Dressing (recipe follows)

1- Line a platter or tray with grape or lettuce leaves. Arrange fruit in individual mounds on leaves. Brush avocado slices with lemon juice. Cover and refrigerate until well chilled. Serve with dressing.

SERVES **6**.

HONEY-YOGURT DRESSING

○

¾ cup plain nonfat yogurt

1 tablespoon mayonnaise

1 tablespoon honey

1 to 2 teaspoons poppy seeds

Dash of ground nutmeg

1- In a small bowl stir together all ingredients. Cover and refrigerate until well chilled.

MAKES ABOUT **1** CUP.

MACÉDOINE OF FRUIT

○

A sophisticated version of fruit cocktail. Serve as a salad or as a light dessert. For fun, serve in large oversized wine glasses.

2 red apples, unpeeled, cored, and diced

2 bananas, sliced

1 cup fresh peaches, sliced

1 cup cantaloupe balls or pieces

Juice of 2 oranges

1 tablespoon vodka

½ cup confectioners sugar

Mint leaves, for garnish

1- Place all fruit in a medium bowl. Blend orange juice, vodka, and sugar and mix with fruit. Refrigerate for several hours. Serve in sherbet dishes or large wine glasses with some of the juice. Garnish with mint leaves.

SERVES *6*.

VARIATION:

Substitute apple juice for vodka.

MELON FRUIT SALAD
○

The varied flavors of seasonal fresh fruit and cheese makes an appealing summer salad.

1 cup shredded head lettuce

1 cup cantaloupe balls

1 cup watermelon balls

1 banana, sliced

1 tablespoon lemon juice

1 cup fresh pineapple, cut in chunks

1 cup sliced fresh strawberries

⅓ cup mayonnaise

1 cup grated Swiss cheese

1- Place lettuce in a medium glass bowl. Add melon balls. Sprinkle banana with lemon juice and add on top of balls. Add pineapple chunks and strawberries. Do not stir. Spread mayonnaise on top. Sprinkle on cheese. Refrigerate several hours before serving.

SERVES *6*.

SALAD DRESSINGS

●

Homemade dressings are
far superior to purchased product dressings and they
are easy to make. Most salad dressings can be safely
stored up to a week in the refrigerator. Choose a dressing that complements the salad ingredients.

SEVÉ'S FRENCH DRESSING

A just-right balance of contrasting flavors makes this sweet-and-sour dressing good on any green salad. It is also delicious on a salad of avocado and fresh grapefruit.

⅔ cup catsup
⅔ cup vegetable oil
¼ cup honey
¼ cup cider vinegar
¼ teaspoon Worcestershire sauce
1 teaspoon fresh lemon juice
¼ teaspoon salt

1- Combine all ingredients in a jar with tight-fitting lid, shake well, and refrigerate. Shake well before using.

MAKES ABOUT **2** CUPS.

OREGON BLUE CHEESE DRESSING

Use this creamy dressing with chunks of blue cheese on any combination of greens and vegetables.

¾ cup mayonnaise
½ cup plain nonfat yogurt
3 ounces blue cheese, crumbled
2 cloves garlic, minced
¼ teaspoon Worcestershire sauce
1 teaspoon fresh lemon juice
¼ teaspoon salt

1- In a small bowl stir together all ingredients until well mixed. Cover and refrigerate.

MAKES ABOUT **1 1/4** CUPS.

HONEY-MUSTARD DRESSING
o

Serve with mixed crisp greens. Also good to baste on broiled fish and chicken.

2 tablespoons honey

2 tablespoons white wine vinegar

½ cup mayonnaise

1 teaspoon Dijon mustard

1 tablespoon chopped fresh parsley

¼ cup vegetable oil

Salt and pepper to taste

1- In a small pan over low heat, stir together honey and vinegar until honey dissolves. Cool slightly and whisk in mayonnaise, mustard, and parsley. Gradually whisk in oil. Season with salt and pepper. Transfer to bowl, cover, and refrigerate.

MAKES ABOUT *1* CUP.

CREAMY ITALIAN DRESSING
o

¼ cup olive oil

½ cup mayonnaise

½ cup buttermilk

1 tablespoon fresh lemon juice

¼ teaspoon dried basil, crumbled

¼ teaspoon dried rosemary, crumbled

¼ teaspoon dried oregano, crumbled

¼ teaspoon garlic powder

¼ teaspoon salt

Freshly ground pepper to taste

1- In a bowl whisk together all ingredients until well mixed. Cover and refrigerate.

MAKES ABOUT *1 1/4* CUPS.

GREEN GODDESS DRESSING
o

A variation on the original Green Goddess dressing, which was created during the Roaring Twenties at San Francisco's Palace Hotel.

¾ cup mayonnaise

¼ cup plain nonfat yogurt

1 green onion, including some tender green tops, cut up

1 clove garlic, cut up

2 fresh parsley sprigs, cut up

2 tablespoons tarragon vinegar, or 2 tablespoons white
   wine vinegar and ¼ teaspoon dried tarragon, crumbled

1 tablespoon anchovy paste (optional)

1 teaspoon fresh lemon juice

¼ teaspoon salt

1- In food processor or blender, combine all ingredients. Process until well blended. Cover and refrigerate.

MAKES ABOUT *1* CUP.

REED'S OWN DRESSING
o

My husband, Reed, has a tendency to dump in everything when he cooks. This is his creation—a highly seasoned dressing that is good on pasta salads, green salads, and for marinating cooked vegetables.

¼ cup vegetable oil

¼ cup olive oil

3 tablespoons red wine vinegar

2 cloves garlic, cut up

1 green onion, including some tender green tops,
    cut up

2 fresh parsley sprigs, cut up

¼ teaspoon salt

¼ teaspoon dried thyme

¼ teaspoon dried oregano

¼ teaspoon dried basil

¼ teaspoon celery salt

¼ teaspoon pepper

¼ teaspoon paprika

1 tablespoon freshly grated Parmesan cheese

1 teaspoon Dijon mustard

1- In food processor or blender combine all ingredients. Process until well blended. Transfer to a jar with tight-fitting lid and refrigerate until chilled. Shake well before using.

MAKES ABOUT *1* CUP.

HORSERADISH CREAM

○

Use freshly grated horseradish, if available, for a stronger flavor. Serve this zippy sauce with roast beef or on cooked beets, beans, or broccoli.

⅔ cup plain nonfat yogurt

1 tablespoon grated fresh horseradish or
   prepared horseradish

¼ teaspoon dry mustard

1- In a small bowl stir together all ingredients until well mixed. Cover and chill well before using.

MAKES ABOUT *3/4* CUP.

RASPBERRY VINAIGRETTE

○

Fruit vinegars impart a particularly wonderful flavor to salads. This deep red, sweet-tart dressing tastes as good as it looks on mixed greens and fruits or as a marinade for chicken.

¼ cup raspberry vinegar

¼ cup vegetable oil

¼ cup olive oil

1 tablespoon minced yellow onion

1 clove garlic, minced

¼ teaspoon dried thyme, crumbled

¼ teaspoon salt

⅛ teaspoon pepper

1- In a small bowl whisk together all ingredients until well mixed. Transfer to a jar with tight-fitting lid and refrigerate until well chilled. Shake well before using.

MAKES ABOUT *3/4* CUP.

Pacific Fresh
Thousand Island Dressing
○

Serve this on a salad of small cooked shrimp and avocado slices or with other seafood salads.

1 cup mayonnaise

¼ cup bottled chili sauce

1 tablespoon fresh lemon juice

1 teaspoon Worcestershire sauce

2 drops Tabasco sauce

1 sweet pickle, cut up

½ celery stalk, cut up

2 fresh parsley sprigs, cut up

1 green onion, including some tender green tops, cut up

1- Place all ingredients in food processor or blender and process until well blended. Cover and chill well before using.

Makes about **1 1/2** cups.

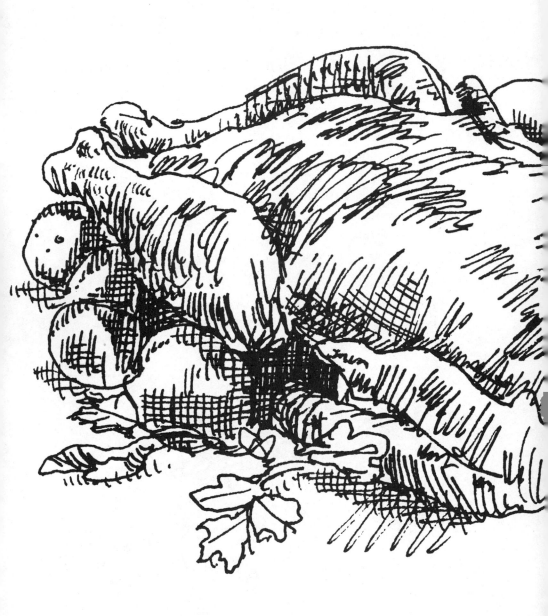

CHICKEN AND COMPANY

○

Poultry is a popular choice
on today's menus because it is relatively low in cholesterol and fat. Besides being a healthful source of
protein, it is economical, readily available, and easy
to prepare in many ways, from roasted, broiled, and
poached to grilled and stir-fried. Poultry is equally
good served hot or cold.

Fresh whole turkeys, turkey parts, and ground turkey
have been appearing with more frequency in markets.
Now this favorite bird is no longer limited to holiday
meals. If you buy a whole turkey and find making
dressing too much of a chore, stuff the bird with
celery, onion, and parsley sprigs or fresh herbs.

I buy whole chickens when they are on special at the
market, and Reed cuts them up so I can freeze them
for later use. As he likes to tell the grandkids, he's an
expert at this because when he was a boy on the farm,

he had to go out to the chicken house, catch a chicken for dinner, cut off its head with an axe, pluck it, singe it, and then cut it up for his mother to fry (in lard, of course).

POULTRY BASICS

Store uncooked poultry in the refrigerator as soon as possible after purchase and cook within 2 days, or wrap poultry in an airtight plastic bag or aluminum foil and freeze for up to 3 months. Label and date the package. Thaw poultry in the refrigerator, not at room temperature. Thawed poultry must never be refrozen.

—

Wash and dry poultry well before cooking to remove any possible surface bacteria.

—

If desired, remove the skin to reduce the fat content further. If all the skin is removed, however, a topping or marinade should be used in preparation to keep the chicken moist during cooking.

—

After working with raw poultry, wash the cutting board, knives, and your hands with soapy water to prevent any bacteria from coming in contact with other foods.

—

Cooking time for chicken pieces is about 1 hour; whole chickens cook in about 1¼ hours. Chicken is done when juices run clear when meat is pierced with a knife near the bone. Chicken breasts take less time to cook and will dry out if overcooked. Test by cutting in the center with a sharp knife; the meat should be white.

—

Allow ¾ to 1 pound bone-in chicken per serving. A 3½- to 4-pound chicken or 1½ to 2 pounds boned and skinned chicken breasts will serve 4.

CHICKEN BREASTS AND MUSHROOMS IN LEMON SAUCE

○

Keep your guests entertained with a glass of wine while you prepare this last-minute dish. Better yet, invite them into the kitchen to watch how easy this lemony-chicken preparation goes together. Serve with rice or plain pasta to absorb some of the delicious sauce.

5 tablespoons butter or margarine

¾ pound fresh mushrooms, thickly sliced

6 green onions, including some tender green tops, sliced

2 cloves garlic, minced

¼ cup all-purpose flour

⅛ teaspoon white pepper

½ teaspoon salt

¼ teaspoon paprika

8 boned and skinned chicken breast halves

¼ cup dry white wine

Juice of 1 lemon

2 tablespoons chopped fresh parsley

1- In a pan over medium heat, melt 2 tablespoons of the butter. Add the mushrooms, onions, and garlic and sauté until slightly soft, about 5 minutes. Remove with a slotted spoon to a plate.

2- In a plate or on a piece of waxed paper, mix together the flour, pepper, salt, and paprika. Dust chicken pieces with flour mixture, coating evenly.

3- Add the remaining 3 tablespoons butter to pan and melt over medium heat. Add the chicken pieces and brown on all sides, turning frequently, about 15 minutes. Remove to plate holding mushroom mixture. Add wine and lemon juice to pan and bring to a boil. Stir with wooden spoon to loosen browned bits and then reduce liquid by one fourth, about 1 minute.

4- Return mushroom mixture and chicken to pan. Reduce heat to low, cover, and cook until chicken is tender and juices run clear, 8 to 10 minutes. Add parsley and serve immediately.

SERVES *4* TO *6*.

ORANGE CHICKEN WITH ALMONDS
○

An easy company dish with a tasty orange sauce. Serve with Mushroom-Leek-Rice Pilaf (page 262) and marinated tomatoes.

    8 boned and skinned chicken breast halves
    Salt and freshly ground pepper to taste
    1 tablespoon butter or margarine
    1 tablespoon vegetable oil
    Orange Sauce (recipe follows)
    ¼ cup slivered blanched almonds
    1 orange, sliced, for garnish

1- Preheat oven to 350°F. Season chicken with salt and pepper.

2- In a large skillet over medium heat, melt butter with oil. Add chicken and brown on all sides, turning frequently, about 15 minutes. As chicken is browned, remove to an oiled 2-quart baking dish. Cover and bake 20 minutes.

3- While chicken is baking, make Orange Sauce. Uncover chicken and pour sauce evenly over top. Bake, uncovered, until chicken is tender and juices run clear, about 25 minutes longer.

4- Transfer to a warmed platter and spoon sauce and juices over chicken. Sprinkle with almonds and garnish with orange slices. Serve immediately.

SERVES *4*.

ORANGE SAUCE

1 cup fresh orange juice

½ cup chicken broth

¼ teaspoon dried rosemary, crumbled

2 tablespoons sugar

¼ teaspoon salt

1½ tablespoons cornstarch

¼ cup dry white wine

1- In a small saucepan combine all ingredients. Bring to a boil, stirring constantly, and boil until thickened, about 3 minutes.

MAKES ABOUT *1 3/4* CUPS.

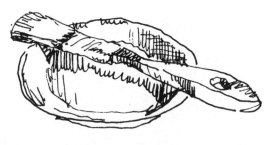

CHICKEN WITH CHILIES AND CHEESE

○

The chili-cheese topping and avocado garnish give this festive dish a Mexican accent.

6 to 8 boned and skinned chicken breast halves

Vegetable oil, for brushing on chicken

Salt and freshly ground pepper to taste

1 cup grated Monterey Jack cheese

1 can (4 ounces) diced green chilies

½ red bell pepper, seeded and chopped

½ cup chopped green onion, including some
   tender green tops

2 ripe avocados, peeled, pitted, and
   sliced lengthwise, for garnish

¾ cup black pitted olives, for garnish

Sour cream or plain nonfat yogurt, for topping

1- Preheat oven to 350°F. Arrange breasts in a single layer in an oiled 7½-by-11¾-inch baking dish. Brush lightly with oil. Season with salt and pepper. Cover with aluminum foil and bake 15 minutes.

2- In a bowl mix together cheese and chilies. Uncover and spread cheese-chili mixture evenly on chicken and then distribute bell pepper and onion over chicken. Bake, uncovered, until chicken is tender and juices run clear, about 20 minutes longer.

3- Transfer to a warmed platter and garnish with avocado slices and olives. Pass sour cream in a bowl. Serve immediately.

SERVES *4*.

CHICKEN CHARISMA

○

A good cook and friend says that if a recipe has sour cream, mushrooms, and wine in it, it has to be good. This chicken dish has it all!

4 tablespoons butter or margarine

½ pound fresh mushrooms, sliced

6 to 8 boned and skinned chicken breast halves

½ teaspoon salt

¼ teaspoon dried tarragon, crumbled

1 teaspoon Beau Monde seasoning

1 cup dry white wine

½ cup regular or light sour cream

4 green onions, including some tender green tops,
    sliced, for garnish

1- In a skillet over medium heat, melt 2 tablespoons of the butter. Add mushrooms and sauté until tender, 3 to 4 minutes. Remove mushrooms to a plate. Melt remaining 2 tablespoons butter in same pan over medium heat. Add chicken breasts and brown on all sides, turning frequently, 10 to 15 minutes. Sprinkle chicken with salt, tarragon, and Beau Monde while browning.

2- Pour wine over chicken, cover, and simmer over low heat until chicken is tender and juices run clear, about 20 minutes. Remove chicken to a warmed serving dish and cover to keep warm.

3- Add reserved mushrooms and sour cream to pan juices and stir several minutes over low heat to loosen browned bits and blend sauce; do not boil. Return chicken and any juices that have accumulated to the pan with mushrooms and simmer until heated through, 2 or 3 minutes.

4- Transfer chicken and mushrooms to a warmed platter. Sprinkle with green onions and serve immediately.

SERVES *4*.

CHICKEN BUNDLES
o

Here, chicken breasts are made doubly good by filling them with thinly sliced prosciutto (Italian ham) and Swiss cheese and then baking them in a wine sauce. Serve with your favorite rice dish.

8 boned and skinned chicken breast halves

Salt and freshly ground pepper to taste

8 thin slices Swiss cheese

8 thin slices prosciutto

Dijon-Wine Sauce (recipe follows)

1- Preheat oven to 350°F. Place chicken breasts between 2 pieces of waxed paper and pound with a meat mallet until ¼ inch thick. Remove top paper and season with salt and pepper. Place 1 cheese slice on top of each breast and then top each with 1 prosciutto slice. Roll up each breast piece from narrow end and secure in place with a toothpick. Place in an oiled 7½-by-11¾-inch baking dish. Pour the sauce evenly over the chicken.

2- Bake, uncovered, basting with sauce several times during cooking, until chicken is tender and juices run clear, about 30 minutes. Transfer to a warmed platter and serve immediately.

SERVES *4*.

DIJON-WINE SAUCE
o

½ cup dry white wine

1 tablespoon Dijon mustard

1 tablespoon firmly packed brown sugar

2 tablespoons butter or margarine

¼ teaspoon salt

1- In a small pan over low heat, combine all ingredients. Stir until sugar dissolves, butter melts, and ingredients are blended, 1 to 2 minutes.

MAKES ABOUT *1/2* CUP.

BAKED CHICKEN WITH HONEY-MUSTARD GLAZE

○

*Just spread this tasty mixture on a quartered chicken, slip it in the oven,
and in an hour you will have a shiny glazed bird, baked to perfection.*

2 cloves garlic, halved

2 green onions, including some tender green tops, cut up

4 fresh parsley sprigs, cut up

½ cup prepared mustard

¼ cup honey

2 tablespoons vegetable oil

¾ teaspoon salt

¼ teaspoon freshly ground pepper

1 chicken, about 3½ pounds, quartered

1- Preheat oven to 350°F. In food processor or in blender combine
all ingredients except chicken. Process until smooth. Place chicken
in an oiled 7½-by-11¾-inch baking dish. Spread glaze evenly on
top of chicken quarters.

2- Bake, uncovered, until browned and juices run clear, about
1 hour. Transfer to a warmed platter and serve immediately.

SERVES *4*.

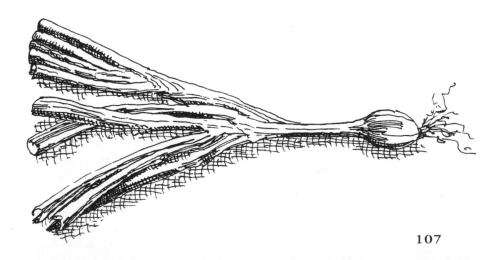

BAKED HERB CHICKEN

○

Local fresh chickens are readily available on the West Coast and are a good choice for any meal. This recipe is so easy it's hard to believe it can be so good.

1 chicken, about 3½ pounds, quartered

2 teaspoons grated lemon zest

Juice of 1 lemon

¼ cup dry white wine

2 tablespoons butter or margarine, melted

½ teaspoon salt

½ teaspoon dried marjoram, crumbled

½ teaspoon dried thyme, crumbled

¼ teaspoon garlic powder

½ teaspoon paprika

Freshly ground pepper

1 yellow onion, sliced and separated into rings

Lemon slices, for garnish

1- Preheat oven to 350°F. Place chicken in an oiled 7½-by-11¾-inch baking dish. In a small bowl stir together all remaining ingredients except onion and lemon slices. Pour evenly over chicken.

2- Bake, uncovered, 30 minutes. Place onion rings on top of chicken and baste with pan juices. Bake, uncovered, until juices run clear, about 35 minutes longer. Baste again before serving.

3- Transfer chicken to a warmed platter. Garnish with lemon slices and serve immediately.

SERVES *4*.

TANDOORI CHICKEN
○

This is an adaptation of a classic East Indian dish of chicken and exotic spices. Serve with Curried Lentils (page 263) and pita bread.

2 tablespoons white wine vinegar

Juice of ½ lemon

½ teaspoon ground cumin

1 teaspoon paprika

¾ teaspoon ground coriander

¼ teaspoon ground ginger

½ teaspoon curry powder

½ teaspoon salt

2 cloves garlic, minced

¼ cup chopped fresh parsley

1 cup plain nonfat yogurt

1 teaspoon cornstarch

8 boned and skinned chicken breast halves

Lime wedges, for garnish

Cucumber spears, for garnish

1- In a large bowl stir together all ingredients except chicken and garnishes. Add chicken pieces and turn to coat evenly. Cover and refrigerate for several hours.

2- Preheat oven to 350°F. Place chicken with marinade in an oiled 7½-by-11¾-inch baking dish and bake, uncovered, until juices run clear, about 30 minutes. Transfer to a warmed platter and garnish with lime wedges and cucumber spears. Serve immediately.

SERVES **4**.

Note: This can also be done in an aluminum pan on a covered barbecue grill.

CHICKEN, SNOW PEAS, AND MUSHROOMS STIR-FRY

○

Rapid cooking keeps the chicken moist and juicy and the vegetables tender-crisp. The walnuts add an extra crunch and flavor. Have all ingredients ready before starting to cook.

¼ cup soy sauce

2 tablespoons dry white wine

1 tablespoon cornstarch

1 tablespoon grated fresh ginger, or
    ¼ teaspoon ground ginger

1 clove garlic, minced

1 pound boned and skinned chicken breast halves,
    cut into ¾-inch pieces

4 tablespoons vegetable oil

½ cup walnut halves

½ pound fresh mushrooms, sliced

6 green onions, including some tender green tops, sliced

¼ pound snow peas, ends trimmed

1- In a bowl stir together soy sauce, wine, cornstarch, ginger, and garlic. Add chicken and mix to coat well. Cover and marinate in refrigerator for several hours.

2- Heat a wok or large, heavy skillet over medium-high heat. Add 1 tablespoon of the oil. When it sizzles, add walnuts and stir-fry until nuts are light brown and crisp, about 2 minutes. Remove nuts to paper towel to drain. Discard oil and wipe wok with a paper towel.

3- Reheat wok over medium-high heat and add another tablespoon of oil. When it sizzles, remove chicken from marinade with a slotted spoon, reserving marinade, and add chicken to wok. Stir-fry until chicken turns white, about 4 minutes. Remove chicken to a plate.

4- Add the remaining 2 tablespoons oil and heat until it sizzles. Reduce heat to medium, add mushrooms and onions, and stir-fry about 2 minutes. Add snow peas and stir-fry until vegetables are tender-crisp, about 3 minutes. Return chicken and reserved marinade to wok. Stir until sauce thickens and all ingredients are heated through, about 1 minute. Add walnuts and mix well.

5- Transfer to a warmed platter and serve immediately.

SERVES **4**.

CHICKEN FAJITAS
o

Now you can make this popular Mexican dish at home and have it taste just as good or better than at a restaurant. Serve with assorted toppings.

> 1½ pounds boned and skinned chicken breast halves,
> cut into long strips ½ inch wide
>
> Fajita Marinade (recipe follows)
>
> 12 flour tortillas
>
> 2 to 3 tablespoons vegetable oil
>
> 1 red bell pepper, seeded and cut into long,
> narrow strips
>
> 1 green bell pepper, seeded and cut into long,
> narrow strips
>
> 1 yellow bell pepper, seeded and cut into
> long, narrow strips
>
> 1 yellow onion, sliced
>
> Toppings: Easy Refried Beans (recipe follows);
> Chunky Guacamole (recipe follows);
> sour cream and plain nonfat yogurt, or a mixture;
> chopped black olives; chopped tomatoes;
> salsa of your choice.

1- Place chicken in a bowl. Add all but 2 tablespoons of the marinade and mix well to coat evenly. Cover and marinate in refrigerator 2 to 3 hours.

2- Preheat oven to 300°F. Wrap tortillas in aluminum foil and place in oven while preparing the fajitas. Using a slotted spoon remove chicken from marinade. In a large skillet over medium heat, warm 1 tablespoon of the oil. Add chicken and sauté, stirring constantly, until chicken turns white, 5 to 6 minutes. Using a slotted spoon remove chicken to a plate; keep warm in oven. Discard any juices that accumulate in pan.

3- Add 1 tablespoon of the oil to same pan over medium heat. Add bell peppers and onion and sauté, tossing and turning until vegetables are tender-crisp, 6 to 8 minutes. If vegetables begin to stick during cooking, add another tablespoon of oil. Add the reserved 2 tablespoons marinade to pan and mix well. Transfer vegetables to a warmed bowl.

4- Serve chicken and vegetables. Place toppings in separate bowls. Let guests assemble their own fajitas by placing some chicken and vegetables in the center of each tortilla, adding toppings as desired, rolling up, and eating out of hands or with a fork and knife.

SERVES *6*.

VARIATION:

Chicken pieces, uncut, can be grilled if desired. Omit sautéing step and grill chicken, turning and brushing with marinade several times, until juices run clear, 15 to 20 minutes. Cut into strips and transfer to a plate to keep warm in the oven until ready to serve.

FAJITA MARINADE
o

Juice of 1 lime
¼ cup dry white wine
¼ teaspoon dried oregano, crumbled
¼ teaspoon salt
⅛ teaspoon freshly ground pepper
¼ teaspoon ground cumin
1 large clove garlic, minced
1 tablespoon vegetable oil

1- In a small bowl stir together all ingredients. Remove 2 tablespoons of marinade and set aside to be added to vegetables. Use remaining marinade for chicken strips.

MAKES ABOUT *1/2* CUP.

Easy Refried Beans

○

2 cans (16 ounces each) vegetarian refried beans

1 cup grated Cheddar cheese

6 green onions, including some
   tender green tops, chopped

1- Preheat oven to 350°F. Place beans in an oiled pie plate and top with cheese and onions. Bake, uncovered, until heated through, about 30 minutes, or prepare beans as directed, cover, and heat in a microwave oven set on high for 5 minutes. Serve immediately.

MAKES ABOUT *4* CUPS; SERVES *6*.

Chunky Guacamole

○

3 ripe avocados, peeled, pitted, and cut up

2 tablespoons fresh lemon juice

2 drops Tabasco sauce

¼ teaspoon Worcestershire sauce

¼ teaspoon chili powder

¼ teaspoon salt

1 small tomato, seeded, drained, and chopped (optional)

1- In a bowl mash avocados slightly with fork. Add all remaining ingredients and mix well. Cover and refrigerate until serving time. Bring to room temperature before serving.

MAKES ABOUT *1 1/2* CUPS.

OVEN CHICKEN PARMA
○

This is one of those great recipes that goes together fast and is easy to prepare. Serve with baked potatoes and a fresh vegetable for a family meal.

¾ cup buttermilk

1 cup fine dried sourdough bread crumbs

½ cup grated Parmesan cheese

¼ teaspoon garlic powder

¼ teaspoon dried basil, crumbled

¼ teaspoon dried oregano, crumbled

½ teaspoon salt

Freshly ground pepper to taste

1 chicken, about 3½ pounds, cut into serving pieces

1- Preheat oven to 350°F. Pour buttermilk into a pie plate. On a large piece of waxed paper mix together crumbs, cheese, garlic powder, herbs, salt, and pepper. Dip chicken pieces in buttermilk and then roll in crumb mixture to coat evenly. Arrange in an oiled 7½-by-11¾-inch baking dish.

2- Bake, uncovered, until tender and browned, about 1 hour. Transfer to a warmed platter and serve immediately.

SERVES *4*.

TURKEY LOAF

o

Low in fat and leaner than ground beef, ground turkey has become a popular and healthful choice for an inexpensive dinner. It is readily available in most supermarkets. Serve this loaf with baked sweet potatoes and cranberry sauce. Makes good sandwiches, too.

1 pound ground turkey

½ large carrot, grated

¼ cup chicken broth

¼ cup chopped yellow onion

1 clove garlic, minced

½ cup dried bread crumbs

1 large egg, slightly beaten

¼ teaspoon dried thyme, crumbled

¼ teaspoon salt

Freshly ground pepper

1- Preheat oven to 350°F. In a bowl mix together all ingredients. Transfer to an oiled 4-by-8-by-2½-inch loaf pan.

2- Bake until lightly browned and crisp around edges, about 1 hour. Remove from oven and let stand 5 to 10 minutes. Run a knife around sides of pan, invert onto a platter, and lift off pan. Slice and serve immediately.

SERVES **6**.

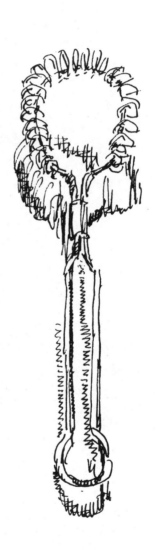

ROAST CHICKEN AND VEGETABLES

o

Gather around the table for this cozy meal of comfort food. Chicken and vegetables are seasoned with oil and herbs and baked together in one pan for an easy oven dinner.

2½ tablespoons butter or margarine

2 tablespoons vegetable oil

2 large cloves garlic, minced

1 teaspoon dried thyme, crumbled

1 teaspoon dried basil, crumbled

½ teaspoon paprika

1 teaspoon salt

¼ teaspoon freshly ground pepper

2 drops Tabasco sauce

1 chicken, about 3½ pounds, cut into serving pieces

3 large new potatoes, about 1½ pounds,
    cut in half lengthwise

1 large yellow onion, quartered

3 large carrots, cut into 2-inch pieces

1 zucchini, cut lengthwise into quarters

1 cup fresh or thawed frozen peas

Chopped fresh parsley, for garnish

1- Preheat oven to 375°F. Combine butter, oil, garlic, thyme, basil, paprika, salt, pepper, and Tabasco in a large roasting pan. Place in oven. When butter melts, mix with seasonings and spread evenly over pan bottom. Add chicken to pan and turn to coat all sides evenly with butter mixture. Turn chicken pieces skin side up. Add potatoes, onion, and carrots, and roll in seasoned butter. Bake, uncovered, 20 minutes.

2- Reduce oven temperature to 350°F and turn vegetables. Add zucchini and bake, uncovered, 30 minutes longer. Add peas and cook until chicken and vegetables are tender, about 10 minutes longer.

3- Transfer chicken to center of a warmed platter and surround with the vegetables. Sprinkle with parsley. Serve immediately.

SERVES *4*.

ROAST CHICKEN DIJON

○

The chicken stays moist in a flavorful sauce of Dijon mustard, wine, and herbs that is good enough for the most special occasion. Serve with Walnut and Bulgur Casserole (page 264) and use the sauce on the bulgur.

1 large chicken, 3½ to 4 pounds

3 new potatoes, about 1 pound, halved lengthwise

3 tablespoons butter or margarine

1 tablespoon Dijon mustard

1 clove garlic, minced

1 tablespoon chopped fresh tarragon leaves, or
    1 teaspoon dried tarragon, crumbled

½ cup dry white wine

Salt and freshly ground pepper to taste

1- Preheat oven to 350°F. Place chicken breast side up in an oiled baking dish. Arrange potatoes around chicken. In a small saucepan over medium-low heat, melt butter; add mustard, garlic, and tarragon and whisk to mix. Whisk in wine and pour mixture over chicken and potatoes. Season with salt and pepper.

2- Bake, uncovered, 30 minutes. Spoon pan juices over chicken and bake until chicken is golden brown and juices run clear, 40 to 45 minutes longer. Spoon juices over chicken again, then remove chicken to a warmed platter. Let stand 10 minutes, then carve.

SERVES *4*.

Note: If a sauce is desired, pour pan juices into a saucepan (you should have about 1 cup). Add chicken broth or water if necessary to make 1 cup and bring to a boil. Mix 2 tablespoons cornstarch with 2 tablespoons water. Slowly add mixture to broth, stirring constantly. Continue to stir until thickened to a sauce consistency, about 2 minutes. Pour into a serving bowl.

MAKES ABOUT *1* CUP.

CORNISH GAME HENS WITH RICE-AND-NUT STUFFING

○

*Serve one game hen per person for an impressive dinner. Add a green
vegetable and a fruit plate for a complete meal.*

4 Cornish game hens

Salt and freshly ground pepper to taste

2 tablespoons butter or margarine

1 cup chopped yellow onion

¼ cup chopped walnuts

2 cups cooked brown rice

3 tablespoons chopped fresh parsley

½ teaspoon salt

¼ teaspoon dried thyme, crumbled

Vegetable oil, for rubbing on hens

⅓ to ½ cup dry white wine

Fresh parsley sprigs, for garnish

1- Preheat oven to 350°F. Season hen cavities with salt and pepper.

2- In a skillet over medium heat, melt butter. Add onion and sauté
until soft, about 5 minutes. Add walnuts and stir to coat. Add rice,
parsley, salt, and thyme and mix well. Remove from heat.

3- Stuff each hen loosely with one fourth of rice mixture. Place
hens breast side up in an oiled 9-by-13-inch baking dish. Rub hens
with oil and pour on ⅓ cup wine. Bake, uncovered, until hens are
tender and juices run clear, about 1 hour, basting with pan juices
and adding more wine if pan begins to dry.

4- Transfer hens to warmed platter or individual plates and garnish
with parsley. Serve immediately.

SERVES *4*.

BAKED TURKEY BREAST WITH APPLE-HONEY GLAZE

○

A great way to cook turkey if you like only white meat. Enjoy for dinner and then use any leftovers for sandwiches the next day.

> 1 bone-in turkey breast, about 3 pounds
>
> Apple-Honey Glaze (recipe follows)
>
> 1 apple, sliced, for garnish
>
> Fresh rosemary sprigs, for garnish

1- Preheat oven to 350°F. Place turkey breast in a small roasting pan. Pour glaze over turkey. Bake, uncovered, 1 hour, basting with juices several times while baking.

2- Cover and bake 30 minutes longer until juices run clear or a meat thermometer registers 150°F. Remove from oven and let stand, lightly covered, 10 minutes before slicing.

3- Transfer to a warmed platter and slice. Garnish with apple slices and rosemary sprigs and serve immediately. Pass the warm pan juices in a bowl, if desired.

SERVES **6** TO **8**.

APPLE-HONEY GLAZE

○

> ½ cup apple juice
>
> 1 tablespoon honey
>
> 2 teaspoons chopped fresh rosemary, or
>   ½ teaspoon dried rosemary, crumbled
>
> ¼ teaspoon dried marjoram, crumbled
>
> ¼ teaspoon dried thyme, crumbled
>
> ½ teaspoon salt
>
> Freshly ground pepper to taste

1- In a small bowl stir together all ingredients.

MAKES ABOUT **2/3** CUP.

CHICKEN CACCIATORE
○

This takes time to prepare, but it is so delicious it is worth the trouble. Just the aroma that floats through the house as the dish bakes is enough to pique the appetite. For the chicken pieces, cut up two whole chickens and use only the meaty pieces; save the remaining parts for making broth and other uses. Serve with a tossed green salad, garlic bread and plain spaghetti or other noodles. Apple Crumb Pie (page 272) makes a great ending.

¼ cup all-purpose flour

½ teaspoon salt, plus salt to taste

⅛ teaspoon freshly ground pepper, plus pepper to taste

4 to 4½ pounds choice chicken pieces

2 tablespoons vegetable oil, plus more if needed

1 cup chopped yellow onion

½ green bell pepper, seeded and chopped

½ pound fresh mushrooms, sliced

1 can (16 ounces) plum tomatoes, coarsely chopped, with juices

1 can (16 ounces) tomato sauce

2 cloves garlic, minced

¼ cup dry white wine

3 tablespoons chopped fresh parsley

¼ teaspoon dried marjoram, crumbled

¼ teaspoon dried thyme, crumbled

½ teaspoon dried basil, crumbled

¼ teaspoon dried oregano, crumbled

Freshly grated Parmesan cheese, for topping

1- Preheat oven to 350°F. On a large piece of waxed paper, mix together flour, salt, and pepper. Roll chicken pieces in mixture to coat evenly. Reserve any remaining flour mixture.

2- In a large nonstick skillet over medium heat, warm oil. Add chicken and brown on all sides, turning frequently, about 15 minutes. As the pieces are browned, remove to an oiled 3-quart baking dish.

3- In the same skillet, add onion and bell pepper and sauté 3 minutes, adding more oil if needed to prevent sticking. Add mushrooms and cook until mushrooms are just beginning to lose juices, 2 to 3 minutes longer. Add to dish holding chicken.

4- In the same skillet over medium heat, add tomatoes and juices, tomato sauce, garlic, wine, parsley, dried herbs, salt and pepper to taste, and any remaining flour mixture. Stir a few minutes to blend. Pour over chicken and vegetables in baking dish.

5- Cover and bake until chicken is tender and juices run clear, about 1 hour. Uncover and season with salt and pepper, if needed. Sprinkle with Parmesan cheese and bake, uncovered, until cheese is melted and golden, about 10 minutes longer. Serve immediately.

SERVES *6*.

CATCH OF THE DAY

○

Here on the West Coast,
because of the proximity to rich fishing waters, we
appreciate the wide variety of fish and shellfish and
seafood that appears daily in most local supermarkets
and fish markets. This is not always true in other parts
of the country.

A few years ago, my husband and I traveled to a small
town in the Deep South to visit the headquarters of a
company we represented at the time. Our bosses asked
us to cater a typical Northwest barbecue for a party
they were hosting for over fifty business associates
from all over the country. We thought this sounded
like fun, so we asked our Eugene sources to fly in four
large whole fresh salmon, a variety of Oregon cheeses,
roasted hazelnuts and walnuts, and a selection of premium Northwest wines. We served Columbia River
Salmon with Cucumber Sauce (page 202), Layered
Potato Salad with Horseradish Dressing (page 71),
North Pointe Salad (page 53), and Fresh Peach Ice

Cream (page 298). Reed barbecued the salmon on an open pit and most guests thought it was wonderful. Some of the local folks, however, would not even taste the salmon, insisting they only ate catfish!

Recent studies have shown fish to be a healthful food that should be included in everyone's menu at least two or three times a week. Besides being high in protein and generally low in fat and cholesterol, other reasons for its popularity are its versatility, flavor, and ease of preparation.

FISH BASICS

Always buy the freshest and best-looking (and smelling) fish in the market. The flesh of cut fish should be firm and moist. Whole fish should have bright skin, clear eyes, and scales tightly attached. There should be no offensive odor.

—

Fish should be eaten the day of purchase. Allow ⅓ to ½ pound per person. Wipe the fish with a damp cloth to remove surface bacteria and then dry with a paper towel.

—

It is important not to overcook fish. Overcooking produces tough, dry results and a loss of flavor and nutrients. Allow 8 to 10 minutes cooking time per 1 inch of fish measured at the thickest part. The fish is done as soon as it begins to flake when tested with a fork and it should be removed from the heat at that point, as it will continue to cook from its internal temperature even off the heat.

HALIBUT CALIFORNIA

○

Here is a West Coast–inspired recipe of succulent, firm halibut com-
bined with California olives, avocados, and cheese. This makes a
spectacular presentation for a company dinner.

¼ cup butter or margarine

2 cloves garlic, minced

¼ cup dry white wine

4 halibut steaks, about 6 ounces each

¼ teaspoon salt

1 ripe avocado, peeled, pitted, and sliced lengthwise

4 slices Monterey Jack cheese

¼ cup pitted sliced black olives (optional)

Paprika (optional)

Fresh herb sprigs, for garnish

1- In a small saucepan over medium heat, melt butter. Add garlic and sauté until soft, about 1 minute. Stir in wine and remove
from heat.

2- Place halibut steaks in a large dish. Pour wine mixture evenly
over steaks, cover, and marinate 30 minutes in the refrigerator.

3- Preheat broiler. Remove fish from marinade, reserving marinade,
and place on broiler pan. Broil 3 to 4 inches from heat about
6 minutes on the first side. Turn and brush with reserved marinade and broil until fish flakes easily when tested with a fork, about
6 minutes longer.

4- Remove from broiler and season with salt. Top each steak with
an equal amount of avocado slices and then a cheese slice. Sprinkle with olives (if using). Return to broiler and broil until cheese
melts, about 2 minutes. Sprinkle with paprika. Transfer to a
warmed platter, garnish with herb sprigs, and serve immediately.

SERVES *4*.

CRISPY OVEN-FRIED FISH
○

Fish with a savory coating baked quickly in a hot oven tastes like fried fish, but with less fat and less mess.

⅓ cup milk or buttermilk

Cornmeal Coating (recipe follows)

2½ pounds Pacific red snapper or halibut fillets,
    cut into serving pieces

1 tablespoon vegetable oil

1 tablespoon butter or margarine

Paprika, for topping

Freshly grated Parmesan cheese, for topping

Tartar Sauce (page 130)

1- Preheat oven to 475°F. Pour milk into a pie plate. On a large piece of waxed paper, spread coating. Dip fish in milk and then roll in cornmeal mixture to coat evenly. Place oil and butter in a 7½-by-11¾-inch baking dish and place in oven. When butter melts, add fish and turn in butter-oil mixture to coat evenly. Sprinkle with paprika and Parmesan cheese.

2- Bake until fish flakes when tested with a fork, 8 to 10 minutes for snapper and 10 to 12 minutes for halibut.

SERVES *6*.

Cornmeal Coating
o

3 tablespoons all-purpose flour

3 tablespoons yellow cornmeal

½ teaspoon dry mustard

¼ teaspoon garlic powder

¼ teaspoon dried rosemary, crumbled

⅛ teaspoon freshly ground pepper

½ teaspoon salt

1- In a small bowl stir together all ingredients until well mixed.

MAKES ABOUT *1/2* CUP.

TARTAR SAUCE

○

1 celery stalk, cut up

2 fresh parsley sprigs, cut up

1 green onion, including some tender green tops, cut up

1 clove garlic, halved

1 sweet pickle, cut up

½ teaspoon Dijon mustard

1 teaspoon fresh lemon juice

Dash of Tabasco sauce

1 teaspoon Worcestershire sauce

¼ teaspoon salt

1 cup mayonnaise

1- In food processor, combine celery, parsley, onion, garlic, and pickle. Process until chopped. Add all remaining ingredients and process to blend ingredients fully. Transfer to a small bowl, cover, and refrigerate until serving, or for up to 3 or 4 days.

MAKES ABOUT *1 1/4* CUPS.

VARIATION:

Use dill pickle in place of sweet pickle.

Note: For a quick tartar sauce, mix together 1 cup mayonnaise, 2 tablespoons sweet pickle relish, and 1 teaspoon fresh lemon juice.

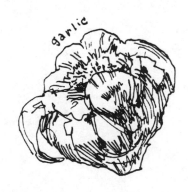

CAJUN BLACKENED RED SNAPPER
○

Blackened fish is not really black. It is just highly seasoned fish that is cooked fast over high heat until well browned. This is spicy hot but absolutely delicious. Serve with ice water! Any variety of rock fish can be used.

1 teaspoon garlic powder

1 teaspoon dried basil, crumbled

1 teaspoon dried thyme, crumbled

¼ teaspoon dried oregano, crumbled

1 teaspoon paprika

½ teaspoon celery salt

¼ teaspoon ground cayenne pepper

½ teaspoon white pepper

½ teaspoon finely ground pepper

½ teaspoon onion powder

2 tablespoons butter or margarine

1 tablespoon vegetable oil

2½ to 3 pounds Pacific red snapper fillets

Salt to taste

1- On a large piece of waxed paper, mix together all seasonings except salt. In a small saucepan over medium heat, melt butter with oil. Brush both sides of fish with some of the butter-oil mixture. Coat both sides of fish lightly with seasonings.

2- Heat a large cast-iron skillet over high heat until a drop of water sizzles on it. Drizzle half of the remaining butter-oil mixture on one side of fish fillets. Place fillets butter side down in pan. Cook on high heat until deeply browned, about 5 minutes. Drizzle on remaining butter-oil mixture and turn over fish. Add more oil if needed. Cook until fish is browned and flakes when tested with a fork, about 5 minutes longer.

SERVES *6*.

CLASSIC POACHED SALMON
o

The salmon is gently simmered in a flavorful cooking liquid and then served with a savory green sauce. Serve with asparagus and Bistro Salad (page 59).

2 cups water

1 cup dry white wine

½ teaspoon salt

1 tablespoon fresh lemon juice

1 tablespoon chopped fresh basil, or
   1 teaspoon dried basil, crumbled

1 tablespoon chopped fresh thyme, or
   1 teaspoon dried thyme, crumbled

1 tablespoon chopped fresh tarragon, or
   1 teaspoon dried tarragon, crumbled

1 bay leaf

6 peppercorns

3 fresh parsley sprigs, plus additional
   parsley sprigs, for garnish

1½ to 2 pounds salmon fillets or steaks

Sauce Verte (recipe follows)

Lemon wedges, for garnish

1- In a 12-inch skillet over high heat, combine water, wine, salt, lemon juice, herbs, peppercorns, and parsley. Bring to a boil. Reduce heat to low, cover, and simmer 5 minutes to blend flavors. Gently slip salmon into skillet. Raise heat and bring to a boil, then reduce heat, cover, and simmer until fish flakes when tested with a fork, 12 to 15 minutes.

2- Remove fish to warm plate and serve immediately with Sauce Verte on the side.

SERVES *4*.

SAUCE VERTE
○

2 green onions, including some
    tender green tops, chopped

4 fresh parsley sprigs

½ cup mayonnaise

½ cup sour cream or plain
    nonfat yogurt

½ teaspoon salt

2 tablespoons chopped fresh dill, or
    1 teaspoon dried dill

Juice of ½ lemon

1- In a small bowl combine all ingredients and stir to mix well. Cover and refrigerate up to 4 days. Bring to room temperature before serving.

MAKES ABOUT *1* CUP.

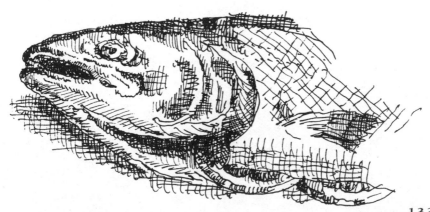

BROILED SALMON FILLETS

○

This is one of the easiest and best ways to prepare salmon. Serve with Dill Butter for extra flavor.

3 tablespoons vegetable oil

1 tablespoon dry white wine

1 tablespoon fresh lemon juice

¼ cup chopped fresh parsley

¼ teaspoon dried tarragon, crumbled

¼ teaspoon salt

Freshly ground pepper to taste

4 salmon fillets, about ½ pound each

Cucumber Sauce (page 203) or
      Dill Butter (recipe follows)

1- In a small bowl stir together oil, wine, lemon juice, parsley, tarragon, salt, and pepper. Place salmon in shallow platter and pour over marinade. Marinate 30 minutes in refrigerator.

2- Preheat broiler. Remove salmon from marinade, reserving marinade, and place on broiler pan. Place under broiler 4 to 5 inches from heat and broil for 4 to 5 minutes. Turn fish over, brush with reserved marinade, and broil until fish flakes when tested with a fork, 4 to 5 minutes longer.

3- Transfer to a warmed platter and serve immediately with Cucumber Sauce or Dill Butter.

SERVES *4*.

DILL BUTTER
○

¼ cup butter, at room temperature

1½ teaspoons chopped fresh dill, or
　½ teaspoon dried dill

1 teaspoon fresh lemon juice

1 teaspoon grated lemon zest (see note)

1 teaspoon Dijon mustard

1- In a small bowl combine all ingredients. Using a fork blend together well.

Note: Zest is the oily, aromatic colored part of the skin of citrus fruits. For best results use a zester, which can be purchased at most cookware stores.

SOLE-SPINACH BUNDLES
o

Delicate sole with a spinach filling, topped with a lemon-wine sauce and served on a bed of spinach, makes an impressive company dish. Add a baked herb tomato to the plate for color, contrast, and flavor.

2 bunches spinach, about ½ pound each, stems removed

¼ cup butter or margarine, melted

¼ cup fresh lemon juice

¼ cup dry white wine

½ teaspoon Tabasco sauce

1 cup cooked white rice

1 cup grated Swiss cheese

¼ teaspoon salt

Dash of ground nutmeg

4 sole fillets, 1½ to 2 pounds total weight

Paprika, for topping

1- Preheat oven to 350°F. In a large covered saucepan over high heat, cook spinach with a little water, until just wilted, about 2 minutes. Toss with a fork once or twice while cooking. Drain well; measure out 1 cup and chop. Leave remaining spinach in saucepan.

2- In a bowl combine butter, lemon juice, wine, and Tabasco. In another bowl mix together the 1 cup chopped spinach, rice, cheese, salt, nutmeg, and half of the lemon-butter mixture.

3- Lay fish fillets dark side up on waxed paper. Divide spinach mixture among fillets. Roll up each fillet from narrow end and place rolls seam side down in an oiled 8-inch square baking dish. Pour on remaining lemon-butter mixture. Sprinkle with paprika.

4- Bake until bubbly, about 20 minutes. Gently heat reserved spinach, stirring constantly, and divide among warmed individual plates. Top each spinach bed with a rolled fillet and serve immediately.

SERVES *4*.

WHITE FISH WITH YOGURT-CUCUMBER TOPPING

○

I was served this seafood dish at a friend's home that overlooks the beautiful Puget Sound in Seattle. My hostess likes to serve easy entrées with no last-minute fuss, so she can enjoy her guests.

> 2 pounds white fish fillets such as sole, halibut, or cod
> Salt to taste
> ½ cup plain nonfat yogurt or light sour cream
> 1 teaspoon fresh lemon juice
> 1 tablespoon mayonnaise
> ¼ teaspoon dried dill
> ½ cup chopped, seeded cucumber
> ¼ cup pitted green olives, sliced
> 2 tablespoons chopped fresh parsley

1- Preheat oven to 400°F. Place fish in an oiled 7½-by-11¾-inch baking dish. Season with salt. In a small bowl stir together all remaining ingredients. Spread evenly over fish.

2- Bake until fish flakes when tested with a fork, 10 to 12 minutes. Transfer to warmed individual plates and serve immediately.

SERVES *4*.

DUNGENESS CRAB CAKES
o

A West Coast version of a southern specialty. The Pacific's wonderful Dungeness crab makes great crab cakes. Look for the Old Bay Seasoning in fish markets and some supermarkets. Serve with Tartar Sauce and/or Red Bell Pepper Sauce.

> 1 pound cooked Dungeness crab meat,
>   picked over to remove shell fragments
> 1 egg, beaten
> 1½ cups finely crushed saltines (about 35 crackers)
> 1 teaspoon fresh lemon juice
> 1 teaspoon Dijon mustard
> 2 tablespoons finely chopped green onion, including some
>   tender green tops
> ¼ cup mayonnaise
> 1 teaspoon Worcestershire sauce
> ½ teaspoon salt
> 1 teaspoon Old Bay Seasoning
> ¼ teaspoon pepper
> 1 tablespoon butter or margarine
> 2 tablespoons vegetable oil
> Tartar Sauce (page 130) or Red Bell Pepper Sauce
>   (recipe follows)
> Lemon wedges, for garnish

1- Flake crab meat into a large bowl. Add egg and ¾ cup of the crushed crackers and mix well. Then add lemon juice, mustard, onion, mayonnaise, Worcestershire sauce, salt, Old Bay Seasoning, and pepper. Mix well and form into 8 crab cakes each about ½ inch thick.

2- On a large piece of waxed paper, spread remaining ¾ cup cracker crumbs. Coat cakes on both sides with crumbs.

3- In a large skillet over medium-high heat, melt butter with oil. Add cakes and cook, turning once, until golden brown, 2 to 3 minutes on each side. Transfer to a warmed platter and garnish with lemon wedges. Serve immediately with Tartar Sauce or Red Bell Pepper Sauce.

SERVES *4* AS A MAIN COURSE, OR *8* AS A FIRST COURSE.

RED BELL PEPPER SAUCE
O

1 large red bell pepper

¾ cup plain nonfat yogurt, drained

1 teaspoon cornstarch

1 tablespoon dry white wine

Salt and pepper to taste

1- Preheat broiler. Cut pepper in half lengthwise and remove stem, seeds, and ribs. Place skin side up on a foil-lined baking sheet with a rim. Broil 4 inches from heat, turning to expose all sides with skin, until evenly charred and blackened, 10 to 15 minutes. Transfer pepper to a paper bag and close the top. Let stand 15 to 20 minutes. Remove pepper from bag and peel off skin. Cut pepper halves into pieces and place in food processor. Add all remaining ingredients and process until smooth.

2- Transfer purée to a small saucepan and place over medium-low heat. Cook, stirring occasionally, until flavors are blended, about 5 minutes; do not boil. Serve warm.

MAKES ABOUT *1* CUP.

SCALLOPS AND MUSHROOMS IN CREAM SAUCE

○

This is a delicious combination of scallops and mushrooms in a perfectly blended sauce. Serve with plain rice, a spinach salad, and warm French bread.

4 tablespoons butter or margarine

1 pound scallops

½ pound fresh mushrooms, sliced

4 green onions, including some tender green tops, sliced

1 clove garlic, minced

½ cup dry white wine

½ cup half-and-half

1 tablespoon Dijon mustard

1 teaspoon fresh lemon juice

¼ teaspoon salt

Freshly ground pepper to taste

¼ cup chopped fresh parsley, for garnish

1- In a skillet over medium or medium-high heat, melt 2 tablespoons of the butter. Add scallops and sauté, stirring constantly, until cooked through, about 5 minutes. Remove with a slotted spoon to a serving dish and keep warm.

2- Return pan to medium heat and add remaining 2 tablespoons butter, mushrooms, onions, and garlic. Cook, stirring, about 3 minutes. Add wine, raise heat to medium-high, and boil until liquid is reduced to about 2 tablespoons, about 2 minutes. Reduce heat to medium, add half-and-half, and cook, stirring occasionally, until slightly thickened, about 3 minutes. Stir in mustard, lemon juice, salt, and pepper and mix well.

3- Return scallops to pan and reheat to serving temperature. Transfer to a warmed serving dish, sprinkle with parsley, and serve immediately.

SERVES *4*.

OYSTERS GOURMET

○

I discovered this recipe years ago at a San Francisco restaurant no longer in operation. The restaurant baked the oysters in a large brick oven, but your home oven or oven barbecue will work just fine. Even if you aren't an oyster fancier, you'll like the sauce, and you just might become a convert! Serve with sourdough bread for dipping in the sauce.

1 pound small fresh shucked oysters,
    drained (see note)

¾ teaspoon dried oregano, crumbled

1 teaspoon dried basil, crumbled

½ teaspoon salt

¼ teaspoon pepper

1 teaspoon minced garlic

2 tablespoons fresh lemon juice

1 tablespoon chopped fresh parsley

6 tablespoons butter or margarine, melted

⅓ cup fine dried bread crumbs or
    finely crushed saltines

Sourdough bread slices, for dipping

1- Preheat oven to 450°F. Place oysters in a strainer and rinse under cold running water. Drain well and arrange in an 8-inch square baking dish. Sprinkle dried herbs, salt, pepper, garlic, lemon juice, and parsley evenly over the top, then drizzle on butter evenly. Cover with bread crumbs.

2- Bake until bubbly, about 10 minutes. Serve immediately in decorative shell dishes or small bowls.

SERVES *4* AS A MAIN COURSE,

OR *6* TO *8* AS A FIRST COURSE.

Note: If small oysters are unavailable, cut larger oysters in half.

STEAMER CLAMS
IN BEER AND GARLIC
○

Serve these clams as a first course with melted butter for dipping and French bread. Fresh clams are generally available the year around with the exception of red tide season, which falls during late July and August. Buy clams that are tightly closed and eat only those that open during cooking.

1 bottle (12 ounces) beer, allowed to go flat

1 cup chicken broth

4 cloves garlic, halved

1 bay leaf

2 fresh parsley sprigs

Salt and freshly ground pepper to taste

50 to 60 steamer clams in the shell, well scrubbed

Melted butter, for dipping

1- In a large saucepan combine beer, broth, garlic, bay leaf, parsley, and salt and pepper. Bring to a boil. Reduce to medium heat and simmer 5 minutes to blend flavors.

2- Add clams, cover, and simmer until clam shells open, 4 to 5 minutes. Remove bay leaf and discard. Remove any clams that did not open and discard. Place clams in 4 large individual bowls and ladle some of the liquid from saucepan over the clams. Accompany with individual bowls of melted butter for dipping. Serve immediately.

SERVES *4*.

SHRIMP WITH GARLIC AND WHITE WINE
○

This popular shrimp entrée, sometimes called scampi, is often featured in better restaurants. I think the chef cooks this dish just so the aroma will tempt your taste buds when you walk in the door. Easy enough to make, you can do this at home.

¼ cup butter

3 cloves garlic, finely chopped

1½ pounds jumbo shrimp, peeled and deveined

¼ teaspoon salt

Freshly ground pepper to taste

¼ cup dry white wine

2 tablespoons fresh lemon juice

3 tablespoons chopped fresh parsley

Fresh parsley sprigs, for garnish

1- In a large skillet over medium heat, melt butter. Add garlic and sauté 2 minutes. Add shrimp and sauté until shrimp turn pink and curl, 2 to 3 minutes. Season with salt and pepper and remove to a warmed serving platter.

2- Add wine and lemon juice to skillet, bring to a boil, and boil 1 minute. Reduce heat, return shrimp and parsley to pan, and heat through. Transfer to serving platter, garnish with parsley, and serve immediately.

SERVES *4*.

PACIFIC FRESH CIOPPINO

o

This Italian fisherman's stew has become a West Coast favorite because it combines the bounty of the Pacific Ocean in one great dish. Serve with a crusty baguette and your favorite salad for a terrific meal.

2 tablespoons vegetable oil

1 large yellow onion, chopped

2 cloves garlic, minced

1 green bell pepper, seeded and chopped

1 can (28 ounces) plum tomatoes,
    coarsely chopped, with juices

1 can (16 ounces) tomato sauce

1 cup dry white wine

1 teaspoon salt

¼ teaspoon dried basil, crumbled

½ teaspoon dried thyme, crumbled

¼ teaspoon dried oregano, crumbled

1 bay leaf

¼ teaspoon freshly ground pepper

1½ pounds white fish fillets such as snapper, flounder,
    or ling cod, cut into ½-inch chunks

½ pound large shrimp, peeled and deveined

16 to 20 steamer clams in the shell, well scrubbed

¼ cup chopped fresh parsley

1- In a large pot over medium heat, warm oil. Add onion, garlic, and bell pepper and sauté until tender, about 5 minutes. Add tomatoes, tomato sauce, wine, and seasonings and simmer, uncovered, to blend flavors, about 15 minutes. Add fish pieces and shrimp and simmer 10 minutes; do not allow to boil. Add clams, cover, and simmer until clams open (discard any that do not open), about 5 minutes.

2- Remove bay leaf and discard. Stir in parsley and transfer to a serving bowl. Serve immediately.

SERVES **6**.

PAELLA

○

*This classic rice dish of Spain is traditionally cooked and served in a
large, shallow, two-handled pan called a paellera. There are many
versions of paella; this one includes most of the traditional ingredients: an assortment of shellfish, chorizo sausage, chicken, vegetables,
herbs, and rice. This dish is not difficult to make, if the preparation
and cooking are done a step at a time.*

½ pound chorizo link sausage,
    cut into ½-inch-thick slices

2 to 3 tablespoons vegetable oil

2½ pounds chicken legs

Salt to taste, plus 1 teaspoon salt

Pepper to taste, plus ¼ teaspoon pepper

1 large yellow onion, chopped

1 green bell pepper, seeded and chopped

1 red bell pepper, seeded and chopped

3 cloves garlic, minced

2 large tomatoes, seeded and chopped

¼ cup chopped fresh parsley

1 jar (2 ounces) pimientos, drained and chopped

2 cups short-grain (arborio) white rice

4 cups chicken broth

¼ teaspoon dried oregano, crumbled

⅛ teaspoon powdered saffron

1 cup fresh or thawed frozen green peas

1 pound large shrimp, peeled and deveined

18 steamer clams in the shell, well scrubbed

¼ cup chopped fresh parsley, for garnish

2 limes, cut into wedges, for garnish

1- In a large nonstick skillet over medium heat, brown chorizo,
turning frequently, for 5 minutes. Using a slotted spoon transfer
to a plate. Add 1 to 2 tablespoons of the oil, as needed, and then

the chicken legs. Brown on all sides, turning frequently, about 15 minutes. Season with salt and pepper to taste. Cover and cook over medium-low heat until tender, about 20 minutes. Remove to plate holding chorizo.

2- Add 1 tablespoon oil to same pan. Add onion, bell pepper, and garlic and sauté over medium heat until tender, about 5 minutes. Add tomatoes, parsley and pimientos and cook 2 minutes. Remove to a bowl.

3- In a large saucepan combine rice, broth, oregano, 1 teaspoon salt, ¼ teaspoon pepper, and saffron. Bring to a boil, reduce heat to low, cover, and cook until rice is tender, about 20 minutes.

4- Meanwhile, preheat oven to 350°F. Transfer rice to an oiled paella pan or 4-quart baking dish. Gently mix in chorizo, sautéed vegetables, and peas. Press shrimp into rice mixture, and lay chicken legs on top. Place clams evenly on top.

5- Bake, uncovered, until clams open (discard any that do not open) and paella is heated through, 20 to 25 minutes. Sprinkle with parsley and garnish with lime wedges. Serve immediately.

SERVES *8*.

VARIATION:

Omit pimientos and add 1 cup pimiento-stuffed green olives with the seafood.

SEAFOOD GRATIN

○

A delightful combination of Pacific fresh seafood covered with a creamy sauce. This makes an outstanding dish for a special occasion—rich and expensive, but very good!

> 6 small sole fillets, about 4 ounces each
>
> ¾ pound scallops, cut in half if large
>
> ¾ pound cooked small shrimp
>
> ¾ pound cooked Dungeness crab meat, picked over to remove any shell fragments
>
> 1½ cups grated Monterey Jack cheese
>
> 2 recipes Hollandaise Sauce (recipe follows)
>
> Fine dried bread crumbs, for topping
>
> Paprika, for topping
>
> Minced fresh parsley, for garnish

1- Preheat oven to 425°F. Lightly butter 6 individual gratin dishes or baking dishes. Arrange sole fillets in a single layer on bottom of dish. Layer on top of each an equal amount of scallops, shrimp, and crab. Top each dish with ¼ cup cheese. Cover each dish with about ⅓ cup Hollandaise Sauce and then sprinkle with a light coating of bread crumbs.

2- Bake until bubbly and tops are lightly browned, 10 to 15 minutes. Watch carefully as they will burn easily. Sprinkle with paprika and parsley and serve immediately.

SERVES *6*.

HOLLANDAISE SAUCE

○

This sauce must be made in two batches in these proportions to turn out successfully. Do not try to double the recipe.

3 egg yolks

2 tablespoons fresh lemon juice

Dash of cayenne pepper

¼ teaspoon salt

½ cup butter, heated but not browned

1- In food processor or blender, combine egg yolks, lemon juice, cayenne, and salt. Process on high speed for 3 seconds. With blender or food processor motor still on high, pour in melted butter in a slow, steady stream, continuing to blend until thick and fluffy, about 30 seconds.

2- To briefly keep sauce warm, transfer to top pan of double boiler or a heatproof bowl and place over a pan of warm water on low heat. Whisk before using.

MAKES *1* CUP.

THE BUTCHER SHOP

○

Meat remains a favorite mainstay
of many of our meals. Nothing can compare to the hearty
flavor of meat or the nutritional value it provides.

In recent years so much has been learned about the fat
and cholesterol in meats that the meat industry has
had to make changes to accommodate these new health
concerns. Breeding and production methods have been
improved, resulting in leaner, better-quality meats. Fat
has been reduced significantly in most meats, especially
pork. On the West Coast, a good range of locally produced fresh meats are delivered to markets daily.

The recipes in this chapter include both old standbys
and some new, intriguing innovations.

MEAT BASICS

When buying beef, select cuts that are well trimmed, have only a small amount of marbling, and are bright red in color. Veal should be creamy pink and very lean. Pork should be grayish pink and fine-grained. Lamb should be pinkish with a velvety texture and a layer of fat around the edges.

—

Allow 5 to 6 ounces per person per serving with consideration for bone and hearty appetites.

—

Refrigerate meat immediately after purchase and cook as soon as possible. If not using within a few days, wrap in aluminum foil or freezer paper, label with date and cut, and freeze up to 6 months for beef and 3 to 4 months for pork. Do not refreeze thawed meat.

—

Wash all surfaces and utensils that have come in contact with raw meat, including hands, with soapy water.

—

To reduce calories and cholesterol, choose lean cuts and cooking methods that do not call for additional fats, such as broiling, pan broiling, roasting, or grilling.

FLANK STEAK WITH HERB MARINADE

○

For an easy dinner, this marinated flank steak can be quickly broiled along with broiled tomato halves and served with Golden Pilaf (page 248).

HERB MARINADE:

    3 tablespoons vegetable oil

    2 tablespoons red wine vinegar

    1 teaspoon Worcestershire sauce

    ¼ teaspoon dried basil, crumbled

    ¼ teaspoon dried rosemary, crumbled

    ½ teaspoon salt

    ¼ teaspoon pepper

    2 green onions, including some
       tender green tops, chopped

    1 clove garlic, minced

    1 flank steak, about 2½ pounds

1- To make marinade, in a small bowl or cup, stir together all ingredients. Place steak in a shallow dish and pour marinade over the top. Cover and marinate in the refrigerator 2 to 3 hours. Remove 30 minutes before cooking.

2- Preheat broiler. Remove meat from marinade. Place on an oiled broiler pan and broil, turning once, 4 to 5 minutes on each side for medium-rare. Do not overcook.

3- Thinly slice on the diagonal and arrange on a warmed platter. Serve immediately.

SERVES *6*.

COMPANY STEAK WITH MUSHROOM-ONION TOPPING

Serve this steak with Buffet Potatoes (page 225), New Caesar Salad (page 60), and Cran-Apple Crisp (page 271) for a special occasion.

1 tablespoon vegetable oil

2 cloves garlic, minced

Freshly ground pepper to taste

4 beef fillets, about 6 ounces each

Salt to taste

Mushroom-Onion Topping (recipe follows)

1- Preheat broiler. In a small bowl stir together oil, garlic, and pepper. Brush mixture on both sides of fillets. Place fillets on broiler pan. Broil, turning once, 5 to 6 minutes on each side for medium-rare.

2- Transfer to warmed platter or individual plates and season with salt. Top with Mushroom-Onion Topping and serve immediately.

SERVES *4*.

MUSHROOM-ONION TOPPING

○

¼ cup butter or margarine

1 yellow onion, sliced and separated into rings

4 green onions, including some tender green tops, sliced

½ pound fresh mushrooms, sliced

3 tablespoons chopped fresh parsley

1 teaspoon Worcestershire sauce

1 tablespoon red wine (optional)

1 teaspoon soy sauce

Salt and freshly ground pepper to taste

1- In a skillet over medium-low heat, melt butter. Add onions and sauté, stirring frequently, 3 minutes. Add mushrooms and parsley and sauté until vegetables are tender, about 5 minutes longer. Add Worcestershire sauce, wine, soy sauce, salt, and pepper and sauté until ingredients are blended, 2 minutes longer.

SERVES *4*.

TENDERLOIN TREAT WITH HORSERADISH MUSHROOMS

○

Although this premium cut of beef is expensive, there is absolutely no waste. It cooks quickly and carves beautifully. Garnish with Horseradish Mushrooms. For a great ending, serve Brownie Cake with Raspberry Glaze (page 281).

MARINADE:

    1 cup beef broth

    1 tablespoon Worcestershire sauce

    1 teaspoon soy sauce

    2 cloves garlic, minced

    2 tablespoons minced yellow onion

    ½ cup dry red wine

    1 whole beef tenderloin, about 4 pounds

    4 slices lean bacon

    Horseradish Mushrooms
      (recipe follows)

    Fresh parsley sprigs, for garnish

1- In a small bowl stir together all marinade ingredients. Place meat in a shallow dish and pour marinade over top. Cover and marinate about 8 hours in the refrigerator, turning meat several times. Remove meat from refrigerator 30 minutes before cooking.

2- Preheat oven to 425°F. Remove meat from marinade, reserving marinade, and place on rack in roasting pan or on broiler pan. Lay bacon on top.

3- Roast until meat thermometer registers 150°F for medium-rare or 160°F for medium, about 1 hour and 15 minutes. During cooking, baste several times with reserved marinade.

4- Remove from oven and let stand 10 minutes before slicing. Arrange slices on a warmed platter and garnish with Horseradish Mushrooms and parsley.

SERVES *8* TO *10*.

HORSERADISH MUSHROOMS

○

20 fresh white mushrooms of uniform size

Vegetable oil

½ cup sour cream

1 tablespoon prepared horseradish

2 teaspoons Dijon mustard

Paprika, for topping

1- Preheat oven to 350°F. Twist stems from mushrooms to remove. Discard stems or save for other purposes. Rub all surfaces of mushrooms generously with oil and place hollow side up on a baking sheet.

2- In a small bowl whisk together sour cream, horseradish, and Dijon mustard. Using a teaspoon fill each cap with an equal amount of sour cream mixture. Sprinkle with paprika.

3- Bake until tender and juicy, 12 to 15 minutes. Serve immediately.

SERVES *8* TO *10*.

STEAK DIANE

○

This is an impressive dish, especially if you have a flambé pan that can be brought to the table. Forget the calories and price for just one meal—this dish is worth it!

4 tenderloin steaks, about 6 ounces each
    and 1 inch thick, butterflied

5 tablespoons butter or margarine

5 green onions, including some
    tender green tops, sliced

½ pound fresh mushrooms, sliced

2 tablespoons finely chopped fresh parsley

½ teaspoon salt

Freshly ground pepper to taste

¼ teaspoon dry mustard

Juice of ½ lemon

1 teaspoon Worcestershire sauce

2 tablespoons brandy

1- To butterfly steak, cut steak horizontally nearly all the way through and lay it flat. In a large skillet or flambé pan over medium-high heat, melt 4 tablespoons of the butter. Add steaks and cook, turning several times, until golden brown, 3 to 4 minutes on each side. Remove to a warmed platter and keep warm.

2- Add remaining 1 tablespoon butter to same pan over medium heat. Add onions and sauté 1 minute. Add mushrooms, parsley, salt, pepper, mustard, lemon juice, and Worcestershire sauce. Stir with a wooden spatula until mushrooms are tender, about 3 minutes. Return meat and any juices to pan holding mushrooms.

3- Warm brandy in a small pan. Light brandy with a long kitchen match and pour over meat and vegetables. When flames die out, transfer meat and vegetables to a warmed platter and serve immediately. Serve on warmed dinner plates.

SERVES *4*.

BEER BEEF ROAST

○

Less tender cuts of beef have a lot of flavor but need moist heat and long, slow cooking. The beer helps tenderize the meat and also adds a tangy flavor. Serve the savory pan sauce over plain pasta.

> 1 cross rib boneless beef chuck roast,
>   2½ to 3 pounds
> Salt and pepper to taste
> 1 yellow onion, sliced and separated into rings
> ¾ cup beer, allowed to go flat
> ½ cup bottled chili sauce
> 2 cloves garlic, minced
> 3 tablespoons all-purpose flour
> ⅓ cup water

1- Preheat oven to 350°F. Place meat in roasting pan and season with salt and pepper. Arrange onion rings on top of roast. In a small bowl stir together beer, chili sauce, and garlic. Pour over meat. Cover and roast until well browned and tender, about 2 hours, basting with pan sauce several times during cooking.

2- To thicken sauce, stir together flour and water. Uncover roast and stir flour mixture into sauce. Bake 5 to 10 minutes longer. Serve immediately.

SERVES **6** TO **8**.

BEEF AND VEGETABLES STIR-FRY

○

Stir-fry cooking is a quick, economical, and healthful way to prepare food. The meat and vegetables are cooked rapidly on top of the stove, stirring and tossing them in very little oil to retain their nutritional value, flavor, and texture. Have all the ingredients assembled before you start to cook. Rice is a natural accompaniment for stir-fry dishes.

⅓ cup soy sauce

1½ tablespoons red wine vinegar

1 tablespoon cornstarch

1 large clove garlic, minced

1 tablespoon grated fresh ginger, or
    ¼ teaspoon ground ginger

1 pound flank steak, cut into
    ⅜-by-1½-inch strips

2 cups broccoli florets

3 tablespoons vegetable oil

½ pound fresh mushrooms, sliced

5 or 6 green onions, including some
    tender green tops, sliced

½ green bell pepper, seeded and cut into
    narrow 2-inch-long strips

2 tablespoons broth or water

1 tomato, seeded and chopped

1- In a bowl stir together soy sauce, vinegar, cornstarch, garlic, and ginger. Add meat, mix to coat well, cover, and marinate in refrigerator for several hours.

2- Bring a saucepan filled with water to a boil, add broccoli, and boil for 2 minutes. Drain well, immerse in cold water to cool completely, drain again, and set aside.

3- Heat wok or large skillet over medium-high heat and add 1½ tablespoons of the oil. When it sizzles, remove meat from marinade with a slotted spoon, reserving marinade, and add meat to wok. Stir-fry quickly until meat is browned, about 4 minutes. Remove meat to a plate.

4- Add the remaining 1½ tablespoons oil to wok. When it sizzles, reduce heat to medium. Add broccoli, mushrooms, onions, and bell pepper and stir-fry about 3 minutes. Add broth and tomato, cover, and cook until vegetables are tender-crisp, about 3 minutes.

5- Return meat and reserved marinade to wok. Stir until sauce thickens and all ingredients are heated through, 1 to 2 minutes. Transfer to a warmed platter and serve immediately.

SERVES *4*.

COUNTRY STEW

o

*This big pot of stew is the centerpiece of our kitchen table for a family
dinner or an informal supper with friends. It is a "no peek" dish that
cooks a long time, filling the air with an aroma to tease the appetite.
Serve with lots of garlic bread, a green salad, noodles, and Chocolate-
Walnut Clusters (page 291) for dessert.*

2 pounds lean beef, well trimmed and
   cut into ¾ to 1-inch cubes

1 yellow onion, quartered

4 carrots, cut into 1-inch pieces

4 celery stalks, cut into 1-inch pieces

1 green bell pepper, seeded and cut into 1-inch pieces

¼ cup quick-cooking tapioca

½ cup fine dried bread crumbs

1 pound whole fresh mushrooms

1¼ teaspoons salt

¼ teaspoon pepper

1 can (14½ ounces) plum tomatoes,
   coarsely chopped, with juices

1 cup dry red wine

1- Preheat oven to 300°F. Combine all ingredients in a large oiled
Dutch oven or 4-quart casserole, stirring to mix well. Cover and
bake 4 hours; do not uncover while baking. Serve immediately.

SERVES **6**.

SALSA MEAT LOAF

The addition of tomato salsa adds a spicy touch to this meat loaf. Serve with roasted potatoes and baked winter squash for a homey meal. Leftovers make wonderful sandwiches.

1 pound lean ground beef

1 cup crushed tortilla chips

¼ cup fresh or prepared tomato salsa

½ cup chopped yellow onion

1 egg

¼ cup tomato juice

¼ teaspoon salt

Freshly ground pepper to taste

Fresh parsley sprigs, for garnish

1- Preheat oven to 350°F. In a bowl stir together all ingredients except parsley garnish until well mixed. Turn into a well-oiled 5-by-9-by-2½-inch loaf pan. Bake until cooked through and browned, about 1 hour.

2- Remove from oven and let stand 5 minutes. Run a knife around the sides of pan, invert loaf onto a platter, and lift off pan. Garnish with parsley. Slice and serve immediately.

SERVES *4*.

PARMESAN-SPINACH MEATBALLS
○

*Browning meatballs in the oven reduces the fat as well as the prepa-
ration time. Adding spinach to the meatballs and baking them in a
flavorful sauce makes an ordinary dish good enough for company. Serve
over spaghetti or rice.*

1 pound lean ground beef

2 tablespoons chopped fresh parsley

1 bunch fresh spinach, about ½ pound, cooked, finely
   chopped, and well drained, or ½ package (5 ounces)
   frozen chopped spinach, thawed, well drained,
   and squeezed dry

2 tablespoons chopped yellow onion

1 egg

1 clove garlic, minced

½ cup crushed saltines (about 10)

3 tablespoons freshly grated Parmesan cheese

1 tablespoon milk

¼ teaspoon salt

Freshly ground pepper to taste

2 cups Quick Tomato Sauce (page 251)

1- Preheat oven to 400°F. In a medium bowl combine all ingredients except sauce and mix well. Shape mixture into 1-inch balls.
Place balls on a rimmed baking sheet.

2- Bake until well browned and partially cooked, 10 to 12 minutes.
Pour off excess grease and transfer to an oiled 2-quart casserole. Pour
tomato sauce evenly over top. Reduce oven temperature to 350°F.
Cover and bake until bubbly, 40 minutes. Serve immediately.

SERVES *4*.

VEAL WITH MUSHROOMS, LEMON AND CAPER SAUCE

o

The addition of mushrooms and rosemary to this dish is a variation on the traditional veal piccata. Serve with Steamed Mixed Vegetables (page 239) and Fall Creek Blueberry Crisp (page 268).

8 veal scallops, about 1½ pounds total weight

¼ cup all-purpose flour

¼ teaspoon salt

Freshly ground pepper to taste

5 tablespoons butter or margarine

½ pound fresh mushrooms, sliced

1 clove garlic, minced

6 green onions, including some
    tender green tops, sliced

¼ cup dry white wine

½ cup chicken broth

Juice of 1 lemon

1 tablespoon capers, drained

1 tablespoon chopped fresh rosemary, or
    ¾ teaspoon dried rosemary, crumbled

2 tablespoons chopped fresh parsley

1 lemon, sliced, for garnish

1- Place veal scallops between 2 pieces of waxed paper and pound with a meat mallet until veal is 1/8 to 1/4 inch thick. On a large piece of waxed paper, mix together flour, salt, and pepper. Dip each piece of veal in flour mixture to coat evenly.

2- In a large skillet over medium heat, melt 2 tablespoons of the butter. Add mushrooms, garlic, and onions and sauté until soft, about 5 minutes. Using a slotted spoon remove to a warmed platter.

3- Add remaining 3 tablespoons butter to same skillet over medum-high heat. Add veal and brown, turning once, 3 to 4 minutes on each side. Remove to platter. Add wine, broth, lemon juice, capers, rosemary, and parsley to pan and cook, stirring to reduce liquid, about 2 minutes. Return veal and mushroom mixture to pan and cook until well blended and heated through, 2 to 3 minutes.

4- Arrange veal on warmed platter. Pour mushroom sauce over top and then garnish with lemon slices. Serve immediately.

SERVES **4**.

Note: Ask your butcher to pound the veal for you.

VARIATION:

Omit veal. Use boned and skinned chicken breast halves, preparing them as directed for the veal.

Veal Saltimbocca

○

A classic Italian dish that is a specialty of Italian restaurants. You can make it at home following these simplified directions.

8 veal scallops, about 1½ pounds total weight

¼ cup all-purpose flour

¼ teaspoon dried sage, crumbled

¼ teaspoon salt

⅛ teaspoon freshly ground pepper

8 slices mozzarella cheese, thinly sliced

8 slices prosciutto (Italian ham),
   thinly sliced

6 tablespoons butter or margarine

½ cup dry white wine

Juice of 1 lemon

3 tablespoons chopped fresh parsley

1- Preheat oven to 400°F. Place veal scallops between 2 pieces of waxed paper and pound with a meat mallet until veal is ⅛ to ¼ inch thick. On a large piece of waxed paper, mix together flour, sage, salt, and pepper. Lay a slice of cheese on each piece of veal. Top with a slice of prosciutto. Roll up veal from narrow end and secure with toothpicks. Roll each piece of veal in flour mixture to coat evenly.

2- In a large skillet over medium heat, melt 3 tablespoons of the butter. Add veal and brown lightly on all sides, about 10 minutes. Transfer to an oiled 2-quart baking dish and bake, uncovered, about 10 minutes.

3- Meanwhile, add wine and lemon juice to same skillet over medium heat. Cook, stirring to loosen browned bits, until liquid is reduced by half, about 5 minutes. Whisk in remaining 3 tablespoons butter, small pieces at a time. When veal has baked 10 minutes, pour sauce from skillet over rolls and return veal to oven to bake 8 to 10 minutes longer.

4- Transfer veal rolls to a warmed platter, remove toothpicks, and pour sauce over top. Sprinkle with parsley and serve immediately.

SERVES *4*.

Note: Ask your butcher to pound the veal for you.

SAUSAGE-CLAM LOAF

○

This combination of ingredients may sound strange, but trust me, this dish is good. Serve hot as a main course or cold for sandwiches or hors d'oeuvres with baguette slices and Dijon Mayonnaise (page 73).

> 1 pound bulk pork sausage
>
> 1 egg
>
> 1 cup crushed saltines
>
> ½ small yellow onion, cut up
>
> 1 can (6½ ounces) chopped clams with liquid
>
> ⅛ teaspoon salt

1- Preheat oven to 350°F. In a food processor combine all ingredients. Process until well mixed. Pack into an oiled 4-by-8-by-2½-inch loaf pan. Bake until browned on top and bubbly around the edges, about 1 hour.

2- Remove from oven and pour off excess grease. Let stand 5 minutes. Run a knife around the sides of pan, invert loaf onto a platter, and lift off pan. Slice and serve immediately.

SERVES *6*.

VARIATION:

Add 1 cup chopped, well-drained cooked spinach to food processor with other ingredients.

HARVEST PORK ROAST

○

The rich sweet flavor of pork is enhanced by fresh herbs and garlic. Roasted with vegetables and fruit, this pork loin makes a traditional fall meal.

3 cloves garlic, minced

1 teaspoon salt

1 tablespoon chopped fresh rosemary, or
   ¾ teaspoon dried rosemary, crumbled

1 tablespoon chopped fresh thyme, or
   ¾ teaspoon dried thyme, crumbled

⅛ teaspoon ground allspice

Freshly ground pepper to taste

2½ tablespoons vegetable oil

1 pork loin roast, 4 to 5 pounds

3 potatoes, peeled and halved lengthwise

4 large carrots, cut on the diagonal into 1-inch pieces

2 small apples, peeled, quartered, and cored

10 dried prunes

Fresh parsley sprigs, for garnish

1- Preheat oven to 400°F. In a small bowl mix together garlic, salt, herbs, allspice, pepper, and oil. Rub mixture over all surfaces of roast. Place roast, fat side up, on rack in roasting pan.

2- Roast 10 minutes. Reduce oven temperature to 350°F and roast about 20 minutes longer. Add potatoes and carrots, cover, and roast 45 minutes longer. Add apples and prunes, re-cover, and roast about 15 minutes or until a meat thermometer registers 160° to 170°F.

3- Remove from oven and let stand 15 to 20 minutes before carving. Carve roast and arrange on a warmed platter. Surround with a border of vegetables, fruit, and parsley sprigs.

SERVES *6*.

PORK AND VEGETABLES STIR-FRY

○

Here is a stir-fry dish that goes together in minutes. Prepare a pot of steamed rice and have all the ingredients ready before you begin to cook the stir-fry.

¼ cup soy sauce

2 tablespoons dry white wine

1 tablespoon cornstarch

1 teaspoon sugar

1 tablespoon grated fresh ginger, or
    ¼ teaspoon ground ginger

1 pound boneless pork, cut into
    ⅜-by-1½-inch strips

3 tablespoons vegetable oil

½ cup chopped yellow onion

1 red bell pepper, seeded and cut into
    narrow 2-inch-long strips

¼ pound snow peas, trimmed

½ pound fresh mushrooms, sliced

¼ cup chicken broth or water

12 cherry tomatoes

1- In a bowl mix together soy sauce, wine, cornstarch, sugar, and ginger. Add meat, mix to coat well, cover, and marinate in refrigerator for several hours.

2- Heat wok or large skillet over medium-high heat and add 1½ tablespoons of the oil. When it sizzles, remove meat from marinade with a slotted spoon, reserving marinade, and add meat to wok. Stir-fry until meat is browned, about 4 minutes. Remove meat to a plate.

3- Add remaining 1½ tablespoons oil to wok and when it sizzles, reduce heat to medium. Add onion and bell pepper and stir-fry about 2 minutes. Add snow peas and mushrooms and stir-fry 2 minutes longer. Add broth, cover, and cook until vegetables are tender-crisp, 3 to 4 minutes.

4- Return meat to wok along with tomatoes and reserved marinade. Stir until sauce thickens and all ingredients are heated through, 1 to 2 minutes. Transfer to a warmed platter and serve immediately.

SERVES *4*.

CHEF'S PORK CHOPS

○

Thick pork chops are baked in a superb mustardy sauce with dill pickle as the surprise flavor. Serve with Barley-Rice-Nut Pilaf (page 255) and California Salad (page 62).

3 tablespoons butter or margarine

1 tablespoon vegetable oil

8 pork chops, about 2 pounds total weight

Salt and freshly ground pepper to taste

1 clove garlic, minced

1 large dill pickle, chopped

6 green onions, including some
   tender green tops, sliced

¼ cup all-purpose flour

2 cups chicken broth

1 tablespoon Dijon mustard

¼ cup dry white wine

⅛ teaspoon salt

1- Preheat oven to 350°F. In a large skillet over medium heat, melt butter with oil. Add chops and brown about 5 minutes on each side. Season with salt and pepper while browning. Transfer to an oiled 9-by-13½-inch baking dish. Add garlic, pickle, and green onions to drippings in skillet and sauté over medium heat until soft, about 5 minutes. Stir in flour and cook, stirring, 1 minute. Add broth, mustard, wine, and salt and bring to a boil, stirring constantly until thickened. Pour over chops.

2- Cover and bake until chops are tender, about 40 minutes. Serve immediately.

SERVES *4*.

LAMB CHOPS
WITH MUSTARD TOPPING
○

For a long time, my husband didn't think he liked lamb because, as a boy on his family's farm, he ate what was called lamb but was actually mature sheep, or mutton. Ever since I introduced him to young lamb, we have had it often. It is especially good prepared on the grill, but can also be broiled. Remember, always buy the best-quality lamb chops available.

½ cup fine dried bread crumbs

2 teaspoons chopped fresh rosemary,
   plus rosemary sprigs, for garnish

2 tablespoons chopped fresh parsley

1 tablespoon Dijon mustard

2½ tablespoons olive oil

1 clove garlic, minced

¼ teaspoon salt

⅛ teaspoon pepper

8 lamb chops, each 1 to 1¼ inches thick

1- Preheat broiler. In a small bowl stir together all ingredients except lamb chops and rosemary sprigs.

2- Place chops on broiler pan 3 to 4 inches from heat. Broil about 6 minutes. Turn chops over and broil 5 to 6 minutes longer. Spread crumb mixture evenly on top of each chop. Broil until lightly browned and chops are medium-rare to medium, about 1 minute longer.

3- Transfer to a warmed serving platter and garnish with rosemary sprigs. Serve immediately.

SERVES *4*.

LEG OF LAMB WITH FRESH HERBS
o

A classic dinner party entrée that will delight your guests. Lamb has such wonderful flavor very little needs to be done to it—just add garlic and a few herbs and enjoy. Serve with Mint Mayonnaise or Mint Pesto.

1 leg of lamb, 5 to 6 pounds

3 cloves garlic, sliced

Juice of ½ lemon

2 tablespoons vegetable oil

1 tablespoon chopped fresh rosemary, or
    ¾ teaspoon dried rosemary, crumbled

1 tablespoon chopped fresh basil, or
    ¾ teaspoon dried basil, crumbled

2 teaspoons chopped fresh thyme, or
    ½ teaspoon dried thyme, crumbled

½ teaspoon salt

Freshly ground pepper to taste

Mint Mayonnaise or Mint Pesto (recipes follow)

Fresh mint leaves, for garnish

1- Preheat oven to 400°F. Using tip of a sharp knife, make slits in meat. Insert garlic slices into slits. In a small bowl mix together lemon juice, oil, herbs, salt, and pepper. Rub over all surfaces of lamb. Place lamb, fat side up, on rack in roasting pan.

2- Roast, uncovered, 15 minutes. Reduce heat to 350°F and continue to roast until done to your liking, 20 to 25 minutes to the pound or until a meat thermometer registers 150°F for medium.

3- Remove from oven and let stand 15 to 20 minutes before slicing. Carve lamb and arrange on a warmed platter. Serve immediately with Mint Mayonnaise or Mint Pesto and garnish with mint leaves.

SERVES *6* TO *8*.

MINT MAYONNAISE
o

¾ cup mayonnaise

3 cloves garlic, cut up

¼ cup firmly packed, coarsely chopped
   fresh mint leaves

2 fresh parsley sprigs, cut up

2 teaspoons fresh lemon juice

1- Place all ingredients in food processor or blender. Process until well mixed. Transfer to a bowl and serve immediately, or cover and refrigerate up to 2 or 3 days. Bring to room temperature before serving.

MAKES ABOUT *1* CUP.

MINT PESTO
o

1 cup firmly packed fresh mint leaves

1 cup firmly packed fresh parsley

2 cloves garlic

¼ cup walnuts

⅓ cup olive oil

2 teaspoons fresh lemon juice

1 teaspoon sugar

½ teaspoon salt

1- In food processor or blender combine mint, parsley, garlic, and walnuts. Process to form a paste (scrape down sides of the bowl, if necessary). With motor running, gradually add oil and blend until smooth. Add lemon juice, sugar, and salt and process just to combine. Transfer to a bowl and serve immediately, or cover and refrigerate. Bring to room temperature before serving.

MAKES ABOUT *1* CUP.

VARIATION:

Spread pesto on lamb chops and grill or broil.

ON THE GRILL

○

Grilling is a favorite way
of cooking on the West Coast, where it can be done
nearly the year around. It is especially popular in the
summer for picnics, barbecues, and casual entertaining. Grilling is generally considered a healthful
method to prepare food because it requires the addition of little or no fat. Almost all meats, seafood, and
some vegetables and fruits adapt well to grilling.

Today, most grilling is done on a covered gas or
charcoal grill. The gas grill is quicker and more convenient, but the covered charcoal barbecue is preferred
for longer cooking and smoking when preparing large
roasts, whole poultry, or whole fish.

GRILLING BASICS

ASSEMBLE THE EQUIPMENT:

Charcoal briquets, if using. Choose the best quality. Charcoal lighter fluid (do not use fuel not intended for barbecuing, as it may leave an aftertaste and can be dangerous).

—

Gas for the gas grill (if possible, keep an extra tank on hand for emergencies).

—

Barbecue tools such as tongs and spatula for turning food, brush or spoon for applying marinade, water to douse any flames caused by fat drippings, insulated mitt, and meat and oven thermometers.

—

A small table nearby to hold tools, serving dishes, and salt and pepper.

—

PREPARE THE GRILL:

Preheat charcoal grill 20 to 30 minutes, until coals are hot and gray; preheat gas grill 10 minutes.

—

Clean grill rack thoroughly with a wire brush.

—

Brush grill rack with vegetable oil or spray with a nonstick cooking spray.

—

For extra flavor and fragrance, soak a few wood chips, fresh herb branches, or citrus peel in water for about a half hour, then add to coals the last 15 minutes of cooking.

—

MARINADES:

Use a marinade on most foods. Marinades play an important part in grilling because they enhance the flavor, seal in the juices, and, in some cases, tenderize meats.

—

Cover and marinate meats in the refrigerator following recipe directions. Remove from refrigerator 30 minutes prior to grilling.

—

Brush foods frequently with marinade during grilling. Never serve leftover marinade that has come in contact with raw meat unless it has been boiled to destroy bacteria.

GRILLING:

Place steaks, chops, and hamburgers directly on an oiled or sprayed (with nonstick cooking spray) grill rack over hot coals 4 to 6 inches from heat. Turn several times until done to your taste. Salt and pepper after cooking.

—

Place chicken directly on prepared grill rack or in an oiled aluminum pan. This pan method keeps the chicken from burning and charring, especially when a sweet barbecue sauce is added. For a crispier result, remove chicken from pan and place on grill rack the last 10 minutes of cooking. Chicken pieces usually take 1 hour to cook, breasts about 30 minutes, and whole chickens 1¼ to 1½ hours, depending on size.

—

Grill fish steaks and fillets in an oiled or sprayed wire-hinged rack, turning several times. The rack keeps the fish in one piece and makes it easier to turn. Cook 8 to 10 minutes to the inch measured at the thickest part. Fish is done when flesh is opaque and flakes easily when tested with a fork. Do not overcook. Overcooked fish will be dry and tasteless. Fish continues to cook after it has been removed from the heat.

—

Grill vegetables and fruit on a prepared grill rack or in a sprayed wire-hinged rack.

GRILLED FLANK STEAK
IN HONEY-SOY MARINADE
○

For a carefree dinner, serve this flavorful flank steak at your next get-together. It cooks quickly and needs little attention. Serve with Hazelnut Salad (page 64), corn on the cob, and garlic bread.

1 flank steak, 1½ to 2 pounds

HONEY-SOY MARINADE:

¼ cup dry red wine

2 tablespoons soy sauce

1 tablespoon fresh lemon juice

1 teaspoon Worcestershire sauce

½ teaspoon dry mustard

1 teaspoon honey

1 tablespoon vegetable oil

1 clove garlic, minced

⅛ teaspoon pepper

1- Place steak in a shallow glass dish. In a small bowl stir together all ingredients for marinade. Pour marinade over steak. Cover and marinate 2 to 3 hours in the refrigerator. Remove from refrigerator 30 minutes prior to grilling.

2- Prepare grill. Remove steak from marinade, reserving marinade, and grill 4 to 5 minutes on each side, turning once, for medium-rare. Brush steak with reserved marinade as it grills.

3- Slice steak thinly on the diagonal and arrange on a warmed platter. Serve immediately.

SERVES *4*.

Note: This flank steak may also be broiled, following the same directions.

GRILLED TOP SIRLOIN
WITH CHILI MARINADE
○

A hot summer evening calls for this easy, informal entrée. Serve with Baked New Potatoes with Red Bell Pepper (page 230), fresh green beans, and a fruit cobbler.

1 top sirloin roast, 2½ to 3 pounds and 1½ inches thick

CHILI MARINADE:

½ cup dry red wine

¼ cup bottled chili sauce

Juice of ½ lemon

1 tablespoon Worcestershire sauce

1 tablespoon soy sauce

¼ teaspoon chili powder

⅛ teaspoon pepper

2 cloves garlic, minced

1- Place steak in a shallow glass dish. In a small bowl stir together all ingredients for marinade. Pour marinade over steak. Cover and marinate 2 to 3 hours in the refrigerator. Remove from refrigerator 30 minutes prior to grilling.

2- Prepare grill. Remove steak from marinade, reserving marinade. Grill, turning several times and basting with reserved marinade, 20 to 25 minutes for medium-rare.

3- Let stand 10 minutes before slicing, then slice and serve on a warmed platter. Serve immediately.

SERVES *6*.

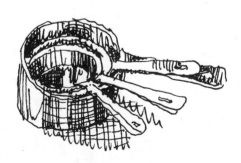

BEEF-VEGETABLE KABOBS
◦

Kabobs are fun to put together and make a colorful and appealing presentation. Serve with a green salad and garlic bread.

KABOB MARINADE:

¾ cup dry red wine

2 tablespoons vegetable oil

3 tablespoons fresh lemon juice

2 cloves garlic, minced

½ teaspoon salt

¼ teaspoon dry mustard

1 tablespoon chopped fresh rosemary, or
  ¾ teaspoon dried rosemary, crumbled

1 tablespoon chopped thyme, or
  ¾ teaspoon dried thyme, crumbled

1½ pounds top sirloin, cut into 1½-inch cubes

10 whole fresh mushrooms, stemmed

1 green bell pepper, seeded and cut into 1-inch squares

1 zucchini, cut into slices ½ inch thick

1 yellow onion, cut into 1-inch wedges and separated

6 plum tomatoes, halved, or
  12 cherry tomatoes (see note)

1- In a bowl large enough to hold the meat, mix together all ingredients for marinade. Add meat and stir to mix well. Cover and marinate for several hours in the refrigerator. Remove from refrigerator 30 minutes prior to grilling.

2- Prepare grill. Remove meat from marinade, reserving marinade, and thread onto metal skewers, alternating meat cubes with vegetables. Grill, turning several times and basting with reserved marinade, 8 to 10 minutes for medium-rare. Serve immediately.

SERVES *6*.

Note: Plum tomatoes are firmer than other tomatoes and do not overcook on kabobs.

GRILLED LIVER WITH GARLIC-BASIL BUTTER

o

Liver lovers have never had it so good! In this recipe, bacon drippings flavor the liver as it cooks, resulting in juicy, tender liver with a delicious smoky taste. You will need a wire-hinged rack to make this dish. Thick liver usually has to be special-ordered, but using it here is important because thin-cut liver will dry out too quickly on the grill. The Garlic-Basil Butter is also good on steak.

> 8 slices lean bacon
>
> 1 yellow onion, cut into rings
>
> 1 ½ pounds calves' liver, 1 inch thick
>
> Salt and pepper to taste
>
> Garlic-Basil Butter (recipe follows)

1- Prepare grill. Lay 4 bacon slices on a wire-hinged rack. Top with half the onion rings, then the liver. Top with remaining onion rings and finally remaining bacon slices.

2- Close rack and place on grill. Turn frequently until liver is browned on the outside and pink in the center, 8 to 9 minutes. Do not overcook. Season with salt and pepper. Serve immediately with Garlic-Basil Butter.

SERVES *4*.

Note: Do not salt liver before cooking, as salt will toughen it.

GARLIC-BASIL BUTTER

○

¼ cup butter, at room temperature

2 large cloves garlic, minced

4 fresh basil leaves, chopped

2 fresh parsley sprigs, finely chopped

1 green onion, including some tender green tops, chopped

1 teaspoon dry white wine (optional)

1- In a bowl stir together all ingredients with a fork until well blended. Cover and refrigerate if not serving immediately. Bring to room temperature before serving.

MAKES ABOUT *1/3* CUP.

GRILLED LAMB CHOPS WITH ROSEMARY

○

A favorite way to grill lamb chops. Allow 2 chops per serving.

1 tablespoon chopped fresh rosemary, or
¾ teaspoon dried rosemary, crumbled

1 clove garlic, minced

1½ to 2 tablespoons vegetable oil

¼ teaspoon pepper

8 lamb chops, each
1 to 1¼ inches thick

Salt to taste

Rosemary sprigs, for garnish

1- Prepare grill. In a small bowl stir together rosemary, garlic, oil, and pepper. Spread mixture on both sides of chops.

2- Stand chops upright on bone end on grill rack and grill 4 minutes. Then lay chops on one side and grill 5 minutes; turn chops over and grill about 4 minutes longer for medium. Watch carefully for flare-ups. Season with salt and transfer to a warmed platter. Garnish with rosemary sprigs and serve immediately.

SERVES **4**.

Mexican Pork Tenderloin with Black Bean Salsa

○

Want an idea for a festive party? Choose a Mexican theme and serve this pork tenderloin marinated with south-of-the-border flavors. Serve with Spanish rice and your favorite chocolate dessert. Set the table with hot colors and matching flowers.

1 pork loin roast, 3 to 4 pounds

ZESTY MARINADE:

½ cup beer, allowed to go flat

Juice of 1 lime

½ teaspoon salt

¼ teaspoon pepper

½ teaspoon dried thyme, crumbled

½ teaspoon dried oregano, crumbled

¼ teaspoon ground cumin

½ teaspoon Tabasco sauce

1 teaspoon Worcestershire sauce

2 cloves garlic, minced

1 tablespoon vegetable oil

Lime wedges, for garnish

Sour cream, for garnish

Black Bean Salsa (recipe follows)

Fresh Tomato Salsa (page 235)

1- Place pork loin in a shallow glass dish. In a small bowl stir together all ingredients for marinade. Pour over pork. Cover and marinate 4 hours in the refrigerator, turning several times. Remove from refrigerator 30 minutes prior to grilling.

2- Prepare grill. Remove pork from marinade, reserving marinade. Grill, turning several times and basting with reserved marinade, until tender and a meat thermometer registers 160° to 170°F, about 1 hour.

3- Let stand 10 minutes before carving. Slice across the grain and arrange on a warmed platter. Serve immediately with lime wedges, sour cream, Black Bean Salsa, and Fresh Tomato Salsa in separate bowls on the side.

SERVES **6** TO **8**.

BLACK BEAN SALSA
o

2 cloves garlic, halved

3 fresh parsley sprigs

2 cups cooked black beans (see note) drained, or
    1 can (15 ounces) black beans, rinsed and drained

1 cup purchased or homemade tomato salsa,
    slightly drained

1- In food processor, combine garlic and parsley. Process until finely minced. Add beans and process slightly. Add salsa and process briefly just to mix. Mixture should be chunky. Place in a bowl, cover, and refrigerate until serving time. Bring to room temperature before serving.

MAKES **3** CUPS.

Note: See Black Beans with Sour Cream and Chopped Tomatoes on page 256. For the salsa, prepare beans only through step where they are simmered until tender. Then remove 2 cups of the beans, drain well, and add to processor.

GRILLED PORK CHOPS
WITH LIME-CUMIN MARINADE
○

Try these Mexican-style pork chops with a tangy flavor. For best results buy thick chops so they do not dry out on the grill. Serve with Black Beans with Sour Cream and Chopped Tomatoes (page 256).

4 boneless pork chops, each
    1 to 1½ inches thick

LIME-CUMIN MARINADE:

    Juice of 1 lime

    ¼ cup dry white wine

    ¼ teaspoon dried oregano, crumbled

    ¼ teaspoon ground cumin

    ¼ teaspoon salt

    ⅛ teaspoon pepper

1- Place pork chops in a shallow glass dish. In a small bowl stir together all ingredients for marinade. Pour marinade over chops. Cover and marinate several hours in the refrigerator. Remove from refrigerator 30 minutes prior to grilling.

2- Prepare grill. Remove chops from marinade, reserving marinade. Grill, turning several times and brushing with reserved marinade, until tender, 12 to 15 minutes. Serve immediately.

SERVES *4*.

ORIENTAL PORK LOIN ROAST
o

For a taste of the Orient, marinate this lean cut of pork in a mixture of soy sauce and seasonings for at least 12 hours or overnight. Accompany with a rice dish.

> 1 pork loin roast, 3 to 4 pounds
> ORIENTAL MARINADE:
>> ¼ cup soy sauce
>> 2 tablespoons red wine vinegar
>> 2 tablespoons vegetable oil
>> 2 tablespoons honey
>> 2 cloves garlic, minced
>> 1 teaspoon grated fresh ginger, or
>>   ¼ teaspoon ground ginger
>> ¼ teaspoon dry mustard
>> 2 tablespoons chopped yellow onion

1- Place pork tenderloin in a shallow glass dish. In a small bowl stir together all ingredients for marinade. Pour marinade over pork. Cover and marinate 12 hours or overnight in the refrigerator, turning several times. Remove from refrigerator 30 minutes prior to grilling.

2- Prepare grill. Remove pork from marinade, reserving marinade. Grill, turning several times and basting with reserved marinade, until tender or a meat thermometer registers 160° to 170°F, about 1 hour.

3- Let stand 10 minutes before carving, then slice across the grain and arrange on a warmed platter. Serve immediately.

SERVES *6* TO *8*.

GRILLED CHICKEN
WITH SPICY BARBECUE SAUCE
o

This spicy brush-on sauce flavors and sweetens the chicken during grilling. Serve with Spinach-Romaine Salad with Pine Nuts (page 56) and watermelon wedges.

> 1 chicken, about 3½ pounds,
>   cut into serving pieces
> Vegetable oil
> Spicy Barbecue Sauce (recipe follows)

1- Prepare grill. Rub chicken pieces with oil. Place in an oiled aluminum roasting pan on top of grill rack and grill 20 minutes.

2- Brush chicken pieces with sauce on all sides and continue to grill, turning several times and brushing with sauce, until tender, 40 minutes longer. The last 10 minutes of cooking, place chicken pieces directly on grill rack to ensure a crispy finish. Serve immediately.

SERVES *4*.

SPICY BARBECUE SAUCE
o

> ½ cup catsup
> 2 tablespoons soy sauce
> 1 tablespoon prepared horseradish
> 1 tablespoon Worcestershire sauce
> 1 tablespoon prepared mustard
> 2 drops Tabasco sauce
> 1 tablespoon red wine vinegar
> 1 tablespoon fresh lemon juice
> ¼ teaspoon garlic powder

1- In a small bowl stir together all ingredients until well mixed.

MAKES ABOUT *3/4* CUP.

GRILLED MUSTARD-ROSEMARY CHICKEN THIGHS

o

These chicken thighs are wonderful for picnics because they are good hot or cold. Pack them into your picnic basket alongside marinated tomatoes, a pasta salad, and buttered rye bread.

8 to 10 chicken thighs,
about 2 ½ pounds

MUSTARD-ROSEMARY MARINADE:

¼ cup Dijon mustard

⅓ cup dry white wine

1 tablespoon vegetable oil

1 tablespoon fresh rosemary, chopped or
1 teaspoon dried rosemary, crumbled

½ teaspoon salt

⅛ teaspoon pepper

2 tablespoons chopped fresh parsley

1- Place chicken thighs in a shallow dish. In a small bowl stir together all ingredients for marinade. Pour marinade over thighs. Cover and marinate several hours in the refrigerator. Remove from refrigerator 30 minutes prior to grilling.

2- Prepare grill. Remove thighs from marinade, reserving marinade. Grill, turning several times and brushing with marinade, until tender and juices run clear, 45 to 50 minutes. Serve hot or cold.

SERVES *4*.

GRAPEFRUIT CHICKEN

○

Grapefruit juice imparts a light and refreshing flavor to grilled chicken. Serve with Grilled Vegetables (page 204) and a mixed green salad.

1 chicken, about 3½ pounds, quartered

GRAPEFRUIT MARINADE:

½ cup fresh grapefruit juice

¼ cup soy sauce

1 tablespoon vegetable oil

2 tablespoons honey

¼ teaspoon ground ginger

2 cloves garlic, minced

1 fresh grapefruit, peeled and divided
   into segments, for garnish

Fresh mint leaves, for garnish

1- Place chicken quarters in a shallow glass dish. In a small bowl stir together all ingredients for marinade. Pour marinade over chicken. Cover and marinate 2 to 4 hours in the refrigerator. Turn once while marinating. Remove from refrigerator 30 minutes prior to grilling.

2- Prepare grill. Remove chicken from marinade, reserving marinade. Grill, turning several times and brushing with marinade, until tender and juices run clear, about 1 hour. Arrange on a platter and garnish with grapefruit segments and mint leaves. Serve immediately.

SERVES *4*.

CHICKEN CHARBONNEAU
o

This chicken is marinated in a robust mixture of beer, mustard, and seasonings and covered with a crunchy coating of sesame seeds. Serve with new potatoes and California Salad (page 62).

1 chicken, about 3½ pounds, cut into serving pieces

CHARBONNEAU MARINADE:

½ cup beer, allowed to go flat

¼ cup prepared mustard

1 tablespoon vegetable oil

2 tablespoons sesame seeds

1 clove garlic, minced

½ teaspoon salt

⅛ teaspoon pepper

½ teaspoon paprika

2 tablespoons sesame seeds, for coating

1- Place chicken in a shallow glass dish. In a small bowl stir together all ingredients for marinade. Pour marinade over chicken. Cover and marinate several hours in the refrigerator. Remove from refrigerator 30 minutes prior to grilling.

2- Prepare grill. Place chicken on grill rack and grill, turning occasionally, 40 minutes. Using the back of a spoon, pat sesame seeds onto chicken pieces, coating evenly. Grill, turning once, until sesame seeds are toasted, 10 minutes longer. Serve immediately.

SERVES *4*.

RASPBERRY CHICKEN

○

The raspberry marinade gives the chicken a pretty rosy glow and an exotic flavor. Serve with Hazelnut-Rice Casserole (page 258).

> 1 chicken, about 3½ pounds, cut into serving pieces
> ½ cup Raspberry Vinaigrette (page 96)
> ⅓ cup dry white wine
> ½ cup fresh raspberries, for garnish

1- Place chicken in a shallow glass dish. In a small bowl stir together vinaigrette and wine. Pour over chicken. Cover and marinate several hours in the refrigerator. Remove from refrigerator 30 minutes prior to grilling.

2- Prepare grill. Drain chicken, reserving marinade. Grill, turning several times and brushing with reserved marinade, until tender and juices run clear, about 1 hour.

3- Transfer to a platter and garnish with raspberries. Serve immediately.

SERVES *4*.

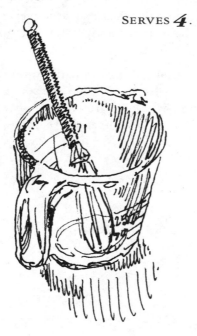

ALL-TIME FAVORITE CHICKEN
o

Always a favorite for friends and family, this barbecue sauce is one of the best.

> 1 chicken, about 3½ pounds,
>   cut into quarters
> All-Time Favorite Barbecue Sauce (recipe follows)

1- Place chicken in an aluminum foil pan. Pour sauce over chicken. Cover and marinate several hours in the refrigerator. Remove from refrigerator 30 minutes prior to grilling.

2- Prepare grill. Place foil pan on grill rack and grill chicken, turning several times, until tender and juices run clear, 50 to 60 minutes. For a crispier finish, place chicken directly on grill rack the last 10 to 15 minutes of cooking. Serve immediately.

SERVES *4*.

ALL-TIME FAVORITE
BARBECUE SAUCE
o

> Juice of 1 lemon
> ¼ cup soy sauce
> ½ cup catsup or bottled chili sauce
> 2 teaspoons Worcestershire sauce
> ¼ cup dry red wine
> 2 cloves garlic, minced
> 1 tablespoon vegetable oil

1- In a small bowl stir together all ingredients until well mixed.

MAKES ABOUT *1* CUP.

CHICKEN-VEGETABLE KABOBS
○

Complete this patio dinner with a pasta dish, a green salad with Oregon Blue Cheese Dressing (page 92), and Chocolate-Walnut Clusters (page 291) for dessert.

KABOB MARINADE:

Juice of 1 lemon

⅓ cup dry white wine

1 teaspoon Worcestershire sauce

¼ cup soy sauce

2 or 3 drops Tabasco sauce

½ teaspoon salt

2 cloves garlic, minced

2 tablespoons vegetable oil

2 pounds skinned and boned chicken breasts,
    cut into 1½-inch squares

1 green bell pepper, seeded and cut into 1-inch squares

1 red bell pepper, seeded and cut into 1-inch squares

1 yellow onion, cut into 1-inch wedges and separated

1 zucchini, cut into ¾-inch pieces

6 plum tomatoes, halved, or
    12 cherry tomatoes

12 whole fresh mushrooms, stemmed

1- In a bowl large enough to hold chicken, stir together all ingredients for marinade. Add chicken and stir to mix well. Cover and marinate several hours in the refrigerator. Remove from refrigerator 30 minutes prior to grilling.

2- Prepare grill. Remove chicken from marinade, reserving marinade. Thread on metal or presoaked bamboo skewers, alternating chicken pieces with vegetables. Grill, turning often and brushing with marinade, until chicken is tender and vegetables are cooked, 20 to 25 minutes. Serve immediately.

SERVES *6*.

WHOLE CHICKEN
WITH WINE-HERB MARINADE
o

This is a delicious general marinade for any type of poultry, especially for whole chicken or turkey.

WINE-HERB MARINADE:

¼ cup vegetable oil

½ cup dry white wine

1 clove garlic, minced

1 teaspoon dry mustard

½ teaspoon Beau Monde seasoning

1 teaspoon poultry seasoning

¼ teaspoon dried sage, crumbled

¼ teaspoon celery salt

1 teaspoon salt

¼ teaspoon pepper

1 whole chicken, 3½ to 4 pounds

1- Prepare covered grill. In a small bowl stir together all ingredients for marinade. Place chicken in an aluminum foil roasting pan and pour half of the marinade over chicken. Place foil pan on grill rack, cover grill, and grill over medium coals (oven thermometer placed on grill rack should register 325°F). Grill, basting chicken several times with marinade, until tender and juices run clear, about 1¼ hours.

2- Let stand 10 minutes before carving, then carve and serve immediately.

SERVES *4*.

BARBECUED TURKEY
WITH CRANBERRY-CITRUS RELISH
o

What a treat! Turkey anytime of the year without all the fuss of making dressing, but you must have a covered barbecue to do it right. The smoke from the charcoal delivers a flavor bonus. Serve with Spinach-Rice Casserole (page 261) and Cranberry-Citrus Relish. Leftover turkey makes great sandwiches.

1 turkey, 12 to 16 pounds
Salt to taste
2 yellow onions, quartered lengthwise
2 celery stalks, cut in half crosswise
Vegetable oil
Dry white wine, for basting
Cranberry-Citrus Relish
(recipe follows)

1- Prepare covered grill. Salt turkey cavity and stuff with onions and celery. Brush outside of turkey all over with oil and place in a large aluminum foil roasting pan. Place foil pan on grill rack, cover grill, and grill over medium coals (oven thermometer placed on grill rack should register 325°F). Allow 20 minutes per pound or until meat thermometer registers 175°F and juices run clear. Baste with juices and a little wine every hour. If turkey becomes too brown, cover loosely with foil.

2- Let stand 20 to 30 minutes before carving, then carve and serve immediately.

SERVES *10* TO *12*, WITH LEFTOVERS.

CRANBERRY-CITRUS RELISH

○

A no-cook relish that is tart and refreshing.

> 1 orange
> 1 lemon
> 4 cups fresh or thawed frozen cranberries
> 2 cups sugar
> ½ cup dry red wine

1- Peel orange and lemon. Reserve one fourth of peel from each fruit and cut up. Cut all of pulp into small pieces and place in food processor. Process briefly. Add cut-up citrus peel and cranberries and process until mixture is chunky. Transfer to a bowl and stir in sugar and wine. Let stand at room temperature for 30 minutes, then cover and refrigerate. May be stored up to 1 week.

MAKES ABOUT *4* CUPS.

COLUMBIA RIVER SALMON
WITH CUCUMBER SAUCE
○

The Pacific Northwest is one of the best-known fishing areas in the country. It is home to the largest and finest salmon, the Chinook or king, which is generally available from early April until October. Other fresh salmon, Coho or silver, are caught from late spring until the fishing season closes. In this recipe the salmon is cooked on a covered grill, which gives the fish a light, pleasantly smoky accent. For a smokier flavor, add a few water-soaked Pacific alder wood chips to the coals the last half hour of cooking.

Mayonnaise as needed

1 whole salmon, 4 to 5 pounds,
   cleaned and head removed

Salt and pepper to taste

1 yellow onion, sliced

1 lemon, sliced

Cucumber Sauce (recipe follows)

1- Prepare covered grill. Spread a thin layer of mayonnaise over the bottom of a large aluminum foil roasting pan. Place salmon on top of mayonnaise. Season the cavity with salt and pepper and tuck in onion and half of lemon slices. Spread mayonnaise on top of salmon and cover with more lemon slices.

2- Place foil pan on grill rack, cover grill, and grill over hot coals (oven thermometer placed on grill rack should register 375° to 400°F), until fish flakes when tested with a fork, 8 to 10 minutes per inch of thickness of fish. (The salmon can also be baked in a preheated 400°F oven, allowing 8 to 10 minutes per inch of thickness.)

3- Serve immediately with Cucumber Sauce.

SERVES *10*.

CUCUMBER SAUCE

○

1 cucumber, peeled, seeded, and diced

2 tablespoons finely chopped
   green bell pepper

1 tablespoon fresh lemon juice

¼ teaspoon dried tarragon, crumbled

¼ teaspoon salt

1 teaspoon sugar

1 tablespoon chopped fresh dill, or
   ¾ teaspoon dried dill

1 tablespoon chopped fresh parsley

¾ cup plain nonfat yogurt

¼ cup light mayonnaise

1- Pat diced cucumber with paper towels to remove excess moisture. Combine cucumber with all remaining ingredients in a bowl. Stir to mix well, then cover and refrigerate up to 2 days. Bring to room temperature before serving.

MAKES ABOUT *2* CUPS.

GRILLED VEGETABLES
○

A convenient way to prepare vegetables is to grill them right along-
side your meat or seafood main course. You'll like the smoky flavor,
but be careful not to overcook. A hinged-wire rack makes turning the
vegetables easy.

1 yellow crookneck squash, cut into
    slices ½ inch thick

1 zucchini squash, cut in half lengthwise

1 yellow onion, cut into
    slices ½ inch thick

2 firm tomatoes, cut in half

8 whole fresh mushrooms, stemmed

BASTING SAUCE:

2 tablespoons olive oil

2 tablespoons balsamic vinegar or
    red wine vinegar

1 tablespoon chopped fresh rosemary or oregano, or
    1 teaspoon dried rosemary or oregano, crumbled

1 clove garlic, minced

¼ teaspoon pepper

Salt to taste

1- Prepare grill. Lay all vegetables in an oiled wire-hinged rack.
In a small bowl whisk together all ingredients for sauce. Brush
vegetables with some of the sauce.

2- Place wire-hinged rack on grill rack over low fire. Grill, turning and basting several times and brushing with additional sauce,
until tender, 8 to 10 minutes; onion will still be somewhat firm.
Transfer to a serving dish, season with salt, and serve immediately.

SERVES *4*.

GRILLED CITRUS HALIBUT
WITH CANTALOUPE SPEARS
○

The combination of lemon and lime juices adds zest to the delicate,
mild flavor of halibut. Grilling the cantaloupe spears intensifies their
natural sweetness, making them a pleasing garnish for the fish.

4 halibut steaks, 1½ to 2 pounds
CITRUS MARINADE:
Juice of ½ lime
Juice of ½ lemon
½ teaspoon grated lime zest
½ teaspoon grated lemon zest
1 clove garlic, minced
1 tablespoon vegetable oil
½ teaspoon dry mustard
¼ teaspoon salt
⅛ teaspoon pepper
½ lemon, cut into wedges, for garnish
½ lime, cut into wedges, for garnish
8 cantaloupe spears, about 1 inch thick, for garnish
Lime Butter (optional, recipe follows)

1- Prepare grill. Place halibut steaks in a shallow glass dish. In a
small bowl stir together all ingredients for marinade. Pour marinade
over steaks. Let stand 10 minutes. Remove halibut from marinade,
reserving marinade.

2- Grill, turning once and brushing with marinade, until fish
flakes when tested with a fork, 4 to 5 minutes on each side.

3- At the same time fish is grilling, grill melon spears, turning
several times with tongs, until warmed, 5 to 6 minutes.

4- Arrange fish on a warmed platter. Garnish with lemon and lime
wedges and cantaloupe spears. If desired, serve Lime Butter on the
side. Serve immediately.

SERVES *4*.

LIME BUTTER

○

¼ cup butter, at room temperature

1 tablespoon fresh lime juice

1 teaspoon grated lime zest

¼ teaspoon dry mustard

⅛ teaspoon Tabasco sauce

1- In a small bowl mix together all ingredients with a fork. Serve at room temperature.

MAKES ABOUT **1/4** CUP.

Note: Lime Butter is also good on cooked asparagus or broccoli.

SHRIMP-AND-SCALLOP KABOBS WITH DILL SAUCE

○

The dill sauce that accompanies these multicolored seafood kabobs will also complement other fish and vegetable dishes. Serve the kabobs with Orange-Gorgonzola Salad with Poppy-Seed Dressing (page 63), Barley-Rice-Nut Pilaf (page 255), and Sour Cream Frosties (page 292).

MARINADE:

¼ cup vegetable oil

Juice of 1 lemon

2 cloves garlic, minced

3 tablespoons chopped fresh parsley

1 tablespoon minced fresh chives

½ teaspoon dried dill

¼ teaspoon salt

Freshly ground pepper to taste

1 pound large shrimp, peeled and deveined

1 pound sea scallops

24 large whole fresh mushrooms, stemmed

1 green bell pepper, seeded and cut into 1-inch squares

½ yellow onion, cut into 1-inch wedges and separated

6 plum tomatoes, halved, or 12 cherry tomatoes

8 slices bacon, partially cooked

Dill sprigs, for garnish

Dill Sauce (recipe follows)

1- In a bowl large enough to hold the seafood, stir together all ingredients for marinade. Add shrimp and scallops and stir gently to mix well. Cover and marinate 30 minutes in the refrigerator.

2- Prepare grill. Remove seafood from marinade, reserving marinade, and thread seafood on metal or presoaked bamboo skewers, alternating seafood with vegetables and weaving bacon strips between and around ingredients. Grill, turning once and basting with marinade several times, until scallops are opaque and shrimp are pink, about 5 minutes on each side.

3- Transfer to a warmed platter and garnish with dill sprigs. Serve immediately with Dill Sauce.

SERVES *6*.

DILL SAUCE
o

¼ cup mayonnaise

¼ cup plain nonfat yogurt

1 teaspoon snipped fresh chives

1 tablespoon chopped fresh dill, or
    1 teaspoon dried dill

1 tablespoon white wine vinegar

½ teaspoon salt

¼ teaspoon pepper

1- In a small bowl stir together all ingredients. Cover and refrigerate until serving or up to 3 days. Serve at room temperature.

MAKES ABOUT *1/2* CUP.

SALMON FILLETS
WITH BASIL PESTO

○

Two summer favorites team up together for a delicious and easy way to grill salmon.

> 1½ to 2 pound salmon fillet
> ¼ cup Basil Pesto (page 247)
> ¼ cup light mayonnaise

1- Prepare covered grill. Lay salmon fillets skin side down on aluminum foil on grill rack. In a small bowl mix pesto and mayonnaise. Spread a light coating of pesto-mayonnaise mixture on top of each fillet. Cover grill and bake until salmon flakes when tested with a fork, 10 to 12 minutes.

SERVES *4*.

GRILLED SALMON FILLET

o

Salmon has such a distinctive buttery flavor, very little needs to be done to it. Here are two easy marinades that particularly complement salmon. Never marinate fish too long in a marinade containing an acid such as citrus juice or vinegar, as the fish will begin to "cook" in the acid.

1½ to 2 pounds salmon fillets

ORIENTAL MARINADE:

¼ cup soy sauce

1 tablespoon vegetable oil

¼ cup dry sherry or dry white wine

1 tablespoon honey

2 cloves garlic, minced

1 teaspoon grated fresh ginger, or
   ¼ teaspoon ground ginger

LEMON-HERB MARINADE:

Juice of 1 lemon

1 teaspoon white wine vinegar

1 tablespoon vegetable oil

2 teaspoons chopped fresh rosemary, or
   ½ teaspoon dried rosemary, crumbled

3 fresh basil leaves, chopped, or
   ½ teaspoon dried basil, crumbled

¼ teaspoon salt

Freshly ground pepper

1- Place salmon fillets in a shallow glass dish. Select one of the marinades and combine the ingredients for it in a small bowl; stir well. Pour marinade over fillets. Cover and marinate 30 minutes in the refrigerator.

2- Prepare grill. Remove salmon fillets from marinade, reserving marinade, and place in an oiled wire-hinged rack. Grill, turning and basting with marinade several times, until fish flakes when tested with a fork, 10 to 12 minutes. Serve immediately.

SERVES *4*.

FROM THE GARDEN

○

In most West Coast supermarkets,
an inviting selection of fresh produce is available every
month of the year. During the summer months, if
you're lucky enough to live near a farmer's market or
roadside stand, you can buy seasonal produce direct
from the grower. Also, backyard gardening has
become a popular hobby in some areas. Today, vegetables play an important part in many cooks' menu
planning. It is not uncommon for vegetables to com-
prise the main course even for nonvegetarians.

VEGETABLE BASICS

Always select the freshest vegetables available, free of blemishes
and firm to the touch.

—

Store most vegetables in the refrigerator in plastic bags and use as
soon as possible. Mushrooms should be stored in a paper bag. Store
onions, potatoes, winter squash, and garlic in a cool, dry place.

—

Wash and prepare vegetables just before cooking. Cook vegetables
only until tender-crisp to preserve flavor and color. Steamers are
excellent to use because they hold the vegetables above the water
so nutrients are not lost.

—

Fresh vegetables have such wonderful flavor, very little needs to be
done to them. Season lightly with butter, a little lemon juice, or a
sprinkling of herbs and salt and pepper to taste. Or, for variety, try
some of the new ways of cooking vegetables included in this section.

ARTICHOKES WITH TWO SAUCES
○

Artichokes grow especially well in the California sunshine from October to July. They are delicious served with individual bowls of melted butter or Hollandaise Sauce (page 149) for dipping or with one of the following sauces. Adding lemon to the water prevents the artichokes from discoloring.

> 4 artichokes
> 4 cups water
> ½ lemon
> 1 bay leaf
> 1 tablespoon vegetable oil
> 4 peppercorns
> Caper Mayonnaise, for dipping
>   (recipe follows)
> Curry Mayonnaise, for dipping
>   (recipe follows)
> Melted butter, for dipping

1- Rinse artichokes under cold water, allowing the water to flow through the leaves. Slice ½ inch off the tops; slice off stems and snap off any lower leaves that are blemished. Trim off sharp leaf tips with scissors.

2- Immediately place artichokes, stem side down, in a saucepan. Add the water, lemon, bay leaf, oil, and peppercorns. Cover and bring to a simmer over medium heat, then cook until tender when pierced and leaves pull off easily, 30 to 35 minutes.

3- Serve immediately with 1 or more sauces of your choice.

SERVES *4*.

CAPER MAYONNAISE
o

½ cup mayonnaise

1 tablespoon capers, well drained and lightly crushed

1 tablespoon white wine vinegar

1 clove garlic, minced

1- In a small bowl stir together all ingredients. Serve immediately or cover and refrigerate up to 1 week. Bring to room temperature before serving.

MAKES ABOUT *1/2* CUP.

Note: This sauce is also good on fish.

CURRY MAYONNAISE
o

½ cup mayonnaise

½ to 1 teaspoon curry powder

1 teaspoon Worcestershire sauce

1- In a small bowl stir together all ingredients. Serve immediately or cover and refrigerate up to 1 week. Bring to room temperature before serving.

MAKES ABOUT *1/2* CUP.

SESAME ASPARAGUS

o

You know spring has arrived when the first asparagus appear in the market. Asparagus only needs to be cooked briefly to retain color and texture.

> 1 pound asparagus
> 1 tablespoon butter or margarine
> 1 tablespoon sesame seeds
> 1 tablespoon fresh lemon juice
> ¼ teaspoon salt
> ⅛ teaspoon white pepper

1- Snap off tough ends of asparagus and discard. Cut spears on the diagonal into 1½-inch pieces. Bring a large saucepan of salted water to a boil. Add asparagus, reduce heat and cook, uncovered, until tender-crisp, about 5 minutes.

2- Meanwhile, in a small skillet over high heat, melt butter. Add sesame seeds and stir until golden, about 3 minutes. Add lemon juice, salt, and pepper.

3- Drain asparagus and transfer to a warmed platter. Pour sesame mixture over top and serve immediately.

SERVES *4*.

GREEN BEANS WITH GARLIC, LEMON, AND BASIL

○

The best green beans are in the market in late spring and early summer. They are wonderful with just butter, salt, and pepper, but try this recipe for extra flavor.

1 pound green beans, trimmed

Juice of ½ lemon

1 tablespoon butter or margarine

2 cloves garlic, minced

1 tablespoon fresh chopped basil, or
  ½ teaspoon dried basil, crumbled

1 tablespoon fresh chopped parsley

¼ teaspoon salt

⅛ teaspoon pepper

1- Bring a large saucepan of salted water to a boil. Add beans, reduce heat and cook, uncovered, until tender-crisp, about 8 minutes.

2- Drain beans well and return them to pan. Add all remaining ingredients, mix well, and cook over low heat 2 minutes longer. Transfer to a serving dish and serve immediately.

SERVES *4*.

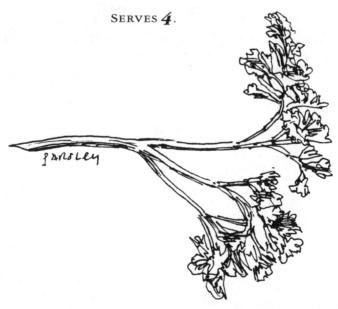

parsley

BABY CARROTS
WITH HORSERADISH

○

Carrots are often under appreciated and ignored. This flavorful, attractive dish will gain them the attention they deserve.

> 1 pound baby carrots
> 2 tablespoons butter or margarine
> 1 tablespoon honey
> ¼ teaspoon salt
> 1 tablespoon prepared horseradish
> Freshly ground pepper to taste
> 3 tablespoons chopped fresh parsley

1- Place carrots on a steamer rack above gently boiling water, cover, and steam until tender, about 30 minutes.

2- In a small saucepan over low heat, melt butter. Stir in honey, salt, and horseradish.

3- Transfer carrots to a warm serving bowl. Add horseradish mixture and pepper and toss to mix well. Sprinkle with parsley and serve immediately.

SERVES *4* TO *6*.

Note: Baby carrots can be purchased in bags, peeled and ready for use, in many supermarkets.

CAULIFLOWER
WITH CRUMB TOPPING
○

A French cook and good friend taught me this recipe. The browned butter and crumbs give the cauliflower a nutty, crunchy flavor.

> 1 cauliflower, broken into florets with ½-inch stems
>
> ¼ cup butter or margarine
>
> ¼ cup fine dried bread crumbs
>
> Salt and pepper to taste

1- Place cauliflower florets on a steamer rack above gently boiling water, cover, and steam until tender, about 10 minutes.

2- Meanwhile, in a small saucepan over high heat, melt butter. Using a spoon stir until bubbly and just beginning to brown, 1 to 2 minutes. Remove from heat. Add bread crumbs and mix until butter is absorbed, about 30 seconds.

3- Transfer cauliflower to a warmed platter. Pour crumb mixture evenly over top. Season with salt and pepper and serve immediately.

SERVES *4* TO *6*.

VARIATION:

Mix 1 tablespoon grated Parmesan cheese with crumbs before adding to butter.

SAUTÉED MUSHROOMS WITH TARRAGON AND MUSTARD

○

Commercially grown mushrooms are a big industry on the West Coast. Equally important and very lucrative is the foraging for wild mushrooms found in the native woods of the Northwest. Mushrooms add flavor and texture to dishes and can be eaten cooked or raw. This is a wonderful way to serve mushrooms as a side dish with meats, especially beef.

1 tablespoon butter or margarine

2 tablespoons olive oil

1 pound large fresh mushrooms, sliced

6 green onions, including some
    tender green tops, sliced

2 cloves garlic, chopped

1 tablespoon chopped fresh tarragon, or
    ½ teaspoon dried tarragon, crumbled

2 teaspoons Dijon mustard

1 teaspoon red wine vinegar

2 tablespoons chopped fresh parsley

1- In a large skillet over medium heat, melt butter with oil. Add mushrooms, onions, and garlic and sauté, stirring frequently, until tender-crisp, 5 to 6 minutes. Add tarragon, mustard, and vinegar and stir until blended, about 1 minute.

2- Transfer to a serving bowl and sprinkle with parsley. Serve immediately.

SERVES **4**.

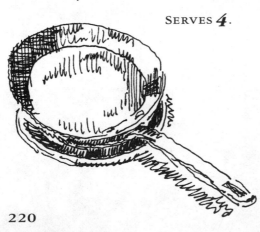

SLOW-COOKED ONIONS
WITH HERBS
o

*Use Walla Walla Sweets from Washington State, if they are avail-
able, for this delectable onion dish; otherwise any dry onion will do.
It is said Walla Walla onions are so sweet and mild, they can be eaten
like an apple! They are also delicious served raw with a splash of
balsamic vinegar. Their season is short and they do not store well, so
use them often when they are in the market in early summer. Serve this
dish with roasts or steaks.*

    2 tablespoons olive oil
    3 large Walla Walla onions or other dry yellow onions,
        sliced and separated into rings
    2 tablespoons dry white wine or water
    1 tablespoon chopped fresh oregano, or
        ¾ teaspoon dried oregano, crumbled
    2 tablespoons chopped fresh basil, or
        1 ½ teaspoons dried basil, crumbled
    ¼ teaspoon salt
    Freshly ground pepper to taste
    2 tablespoons chopped fresh parsley

1- In a large skillet over high heat, warm oil. Add onions, reduce
heat to medium-low, and sauté slowly, tossing and turning frequently, about 25 minutes.

2- Stir in wine, herbs, salt, pepper, and parsley and cook until
onions are translucent and soft, about 10 minutes longer. Transfer to a serving bowl and serve immediately.

SERVES *4*.

SAUTÉ OF SUMMER PEAS AND MUSHROOMS

○

Crisp snow peas, shelled green peas, and fresh mushrooms combine to make a wonderful vegetable dish. Serve with seafood.

4 tablespoons butter or margarine

½ pound fresh mushrooms, sliced

6 green onions, including some tender green tops, sliced

⅓ pound snow peas, trimmed

1 cup shelled fresh peas, or thawed, frozen peas

Salt and pepper to taste

1- In a skillet over medium heat, melt 2 tablespoons of the butter. Add mushrooms and onions and sauté, stirring frequently, until slightly tender and golden, about 3 minutes.

2- Add remaining 2 tablespoons butter to the pan. Add snow peas and sauté about 3 minutes. Add shelled peas and sauté until vegetables are tender-crisp, about 1 minute longer. Season with salt and pepper. Transfer to a serving bowl and serve immediately.

SERVES *4* TO *6*.

BELL PEPPER SAUTÉ

○

A mixture of red, green, and yellow bell peppers makes a colorful accompaniment for almost any meat. Arrange peppers around the entrée for a pretty presentation.

2 to 3 tablespoons vegetable oil

2 cloves garlic, chopped

1 red bell pepper, seeded and sliced

1 green bell pepper, seeded and sliced

1 yellow bell pepper, seeded and sliced

1 yellow onion, sliced and separated into rings

1 tablespoon chopped fresh basil, or
    1 teaspoon dried basil, crumbled

½ teaspoon salt

Freshly ground pepper to taste

1- In a large skillet over medium heat, warm 2 tablespoons of the oil. Add garlic, peppers, and onion and sauté, stirring frequently, until tender-crisp, about 10 minutes. Add more oil if necessary to prevent sticking.

2- Add basil, salt, and pepper and sauté until flavors are blended, 2 to 3 minutes longer. Transfer to a serving bowl and serve immediately.

SERVES *4*.

MASHED NEW POTATOES
AND MUSHROOMS

○

No need to limit mashed potatoes to holiday meals. These mashed potatoes with mushrooms have a sophisticated taste and chunky texture.

4 new potatoes, unpeeled, quartered

½ cup milk

2 tablespoons butter or margarine

8 to 10 fresh mushrooms, chopped

¼ teaspoon salt

Freshly ground pepper to taste

1- Place potatoes in a saucepan with water to cover generously. Bring to a boil, reduce heat to medium, cover, and cook until potatoes are tender but still firm, about 15 minutes.

2- Drain, return potatoes to pan over low heat, and add milk. When milk is warm, using an electric mixer, beat together potatoes and milk. Do not overbeat; potatoes should remain a little chunky.

3- Meanwhile, in a small skillet over medium heat, melt butter. Add mushrooms and sauté until tender, about 4 minutes.

4- Stir mushrooms into potatoes and add salt and pepper. Transfer to warmed serving bowl and serve immediately.

SERVES *4*.

BUFFET POTATOES

This combination of grated new potatoes and sour cream is an unbeatable addition to a meal of roast beef, fresh broccoli, and ice cream with Chocolate Sauce (page 299).

6 new potatoes, unpeeled, halved

1 cup grated sharp Cheddar cheese

½ cup chopped green onions including
   some tender green tops

2 cups light sour cream

½ teaspoon salt

2 tablespoons poppy seeds

Freshly ground pepper

1- Place potatoes in a saucepan with water to cover generously. Bring to a boil, reduce heat to medium, cover, and cook until potatoes are tender but still firm, about 15 minutes. Drain, immerse in cold water, and drain again. Refrigerate to cool completely.

2- Preheat oven to 325°F. Peel potatoes, if desired, and grate in food processor fitted with shredding blade or with a hand grater. Transfer to an oiled, 2-quart baking dish, add all remaining ingredients, and mix well.

3- Bake, uncovered, until potatoes are golden on top and bubbly around edges, about 45 minutes. Serve immediately directly from dish.

SERVES **6**.

ITALIAN POTATO CASSEROLE

○

Serve this savory potato dish with Grilled Lamb Chops with Rosemary (page 187) and California Salad (page 62).

6 potatoes, peeled and sliced
¼ inch thick

1 yellow onion, sliced

3 tomatoes, seeded and sliced

½ teaspoon dried oregano, crumbled

1 teaspoon salt

¼ teaspoon pepper

2 cups grated mozzarella cheese

⅓ cup freshly grated Parmesan cheese

3 tablespoons butter or margarine, cut into bits

1- Preheat oven to 375°F. In an oiled 2-quart baking dish, layer half of the potato, onion, and tomato slices. Season with oregano, salt, and pepper. Sprinkle on half of each of the cheeses. Repeat layers. Dot with butter.

2- Bake, uncovered, until potatoes are tender and top is golden, about 1 hour. Serve immediately or cover and keep warm in the turned-off oven up to 30 minutes.

SERVES **6**.

Note: To grate mozzarella cheese in a food processor, the cheese must be chilled.

SCALLOPED POTATOES AND SPINACH CASSEROLE

○

Scalloped potatoes are true comfort food. The addition of red pepper and spinach makes this recipe special enough for company.

6 new potatoes, about 2½ pounds,
    unpeeled, thinly sliced

½ red bell pepper, seeded and cut into ½-inch squares

2½ cups grated Swiss cheese

Salt and pepper to taste

½ bunch spinach, about ¼ pound,
    dried well after washing

2 tablespoons butter, cut into bits

¾ cup chicken broth

Chopped fresh parsley

1- Preheat oven to 350°F. In an oiled 9-by-13-inch baking dish, layer half the potatoes, bell pepper, and cheese. Season lightly with salt and pepper. Layer all the spinach on top. Repeat potato, bell pepper, and cheese layers, ending with cheese. Season with salt and pepper. Dot top with butter. Pour broth evenly over potato mixture. Sprinkle with parsley.

2- Bake, uncovered, until potatoes are tender and top is golden, about 1 hour. Serve immediately.

SERVES **6** TO **8**.

Spinach

ROASTED POTATOES PARMESAN
o

Prepare these potatoes several hours in advance; then bake in the oven along with chicken for an easy oven meal.

⅓ to ½ cup butter or margarine

¼ cup all-purpose flour

½ teaspoon salt

¼ teaspoon pepper

¼ teaspoon garlic powder

¼ teaspoon paprika

¼ cup chopped fresh parsley

2 tablespoons chopped fresh rosemary, or
   1 teaspoon dried rosemary, crumbled

¼ cup freshly grated Parmesan cheese

6 new potatoes, unpeeled, quartered

1 tablespoon minced fresh chives

1- Preheat oven to 350°F. Place butter in a 9-by-13-inch baking dish and melt in oven. Remove from oven. In a paper bag mix together flour, salt, pepper, garlic powder, paprika, parsley, rosemary, and cheese. Add potatoes and shake well. Roll potatoes in melted butter to coat and arrange in single layer in baking dish.

2- Bake, uncovered, until potatoes are tender and browned, about 50 minutes. Sprinkle with chives and serve immediately.

SERVES *8* TO *10*.

OVEN FRENCH FRIES

○

Hungry for french fries? Bake them in the oven with very little oil and you won't need to worry about the calories. Serve with hamburgers or steaks or as an hors d'oeuvre.

4 large potatoes
2 to 3 tablespoons vegetable oil
Salt, pepper, and Old Bay Seasoning to taste

1- Preheat oven to 425°F. Peel potatoes and place in large bowl with water to cover for 30 minutes to remove excess starch. Drain and pat dry with paper towel. Cut potatoes lengthwise into ¼-inch-thick slices, then cut into ¼-inch-wide strips. In a bowl toss potatoes with oil. Arrange potatoes in a single layer on a baking sheet.

2- Bake, uncovered, 15 minutes. Turn over and sprinkle generously with salt, pepper, and Old Bay Seasoning. Bake until golden brown, about 10 minutes longer. Serve immediately.

SERVES *4*.

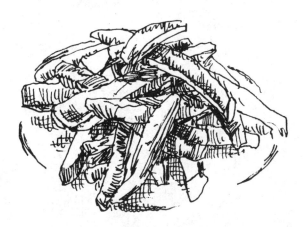

ROASTED NEW POTATOES WITH RED BELL PEPPER

○

Prepare these potatoes several hours in advance and then pop them in the oven for last-minute cooking.

4 large new red potatoes, unpeeled, quartered

½ red bell pepper, seeded and cut into 1-inch squares

½ yellow onion, cut into 1-inch squares

1 tablespoon chopped fresh rosemary, or
   ¾ teaspoon dried rosemary, crumbled

1 tablespoon finely chopped fresh parsley

1 tablespoon snipped fresh chives

¼ teaspoon salt

1–2 tablespoons vegetable oil

Freshly ground pepper to taste

1- Preheat oven to 400°F. Place potatoes in bowl and toss with all remaining ingredients until coated. Place in single layer on a baking sheet.

2- Bake 10 minutes. Turn with a spatula and bake until potatoes are tender, about 10 minutes longer. Serve immediately.

SERVES *4*.

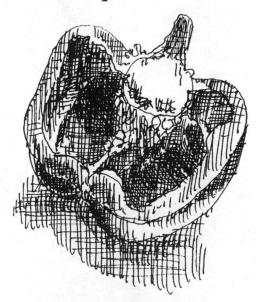

BAKED HERBED TOMATOES

o

Serve these dressed-up baked tomatoes alongside an entrée for color and contrast.

Salt to taste

2 large tomatoes, halved and seeded

½ cup fine dried bread crumbs

3 tablespoons freshly grated
Parmesan cheese

1 tablespoon chopped fresh basil, or
1 teaspoon dried basil, crumbled

¼ teaspoon garlic powder

¼ teaspoon dried thyme, crumbled

Freshly ground pepper to taste

2 to 3 tablespoons vegetable oil

1 tablespoon chopped fresh parsley

1 to 2 tablespoons pine nuts

1- Sprinkle salt on cut side of tomatoes. Turn tomatoes cut side down on paper towels to drain for 30 minutes.

2- Preheat oven to 350°F. In a small bowl stir together bread crumbs, cheese, basil, garlic powder, thyme, pepper, oil, and parsley. Arrange tomato halves, cut sides up, in an oiled baking dish. Spoon an equal amount of crumb mixture on each tomato. Top with pine nuts.

3- Bake, uncovered, until tomatoes are heated through, 12 to 15 minutes; do not overcook or tomatoes will be mushy. Serve immediately.

SERVES **4**.

TOMATOES FLORENTINE

o

Ripe red tomatoes filled with spinach and cheese are so good they deserve center stage. Serve with chicken or seafood.

2 bunches fresh spinach, about ½ pound each,
    or 1 package (10 ounces) frozen spinach,
    thawed and squeezed dry

8 tomatoes

Salt and pepper to taste

½ teaspoon sugar

3 tablespoons butter or margarine

½ cup chopped yellow onion

1 large clove garlic, finely chopped

1 cup coarsely chopped fresh mushrooms

1 egg

½ cup grated Swiss cheese

¼ cup freshly grated Parmesan cheese

1 cup light sour cream

1 tablespoon fine dried bread crumbs

1- If using fresh spinach, in a large covered saucepan over high heat, cook with a little water until wilted, about 2 minutes. Toss with a fork once or twice while cooking. Drain well, pressing out excess water, and finely chop. Set aside.

2- Slice off tops of tomatoes and scoop out seeds and pulp, leaving a ¼-inch shell (save pulp for other purposes). Turn tomatoes cut side down on paper towels to drain for 15 minutes.

3- Preheat oven to 350°F. Arrange tomatoes hollow side up in an oiled baking dish. Sprinkle the inside of each tomato with salt, pepper, and sugar.

4- In skillet over medium heat, melt butter. Add onion, garlic, and mushrooms and sauté until tender, about 5 minutes. Add spinach and stir to mix well.

5- In a bowl beat egg, then mix in cheeses and sour cream. Add spinach mixture and mix well. Divide mixture evenly among tomato shells. Sprinkle with bread crumbs.

6- Bake, uncovered, until tomatoes are tender and tops are lightly browned, about 30 minutes. Serve immediately.

SERVES **8**.

FRESH TOMATO SAUCE
○

The time to make this sauce is when garden-ripe tomatoes are plentiful. The long cooking brings out the natural sweetness and flavor of fresh tomatoes. This full-bodied sauce is good served over pasta, fish, and omelets or added to soups and stews.

½ yellow onion, chopped

2 pounds tomatoes, peeled and cut up (see note)

2 cloves garlic, minced

⅓ cup tomato paste

1 cup water

2 tablespoons chopped fresh basil, or
    1½ teaspoons dried basil, crumbled

1 teaspoon chopped fresh oregano, or
    ¼ teaspoon dried oregano, crumbled

1 teaspoon chopped fresh thyme, or
    ¼ teaspoon dried thyme, crumbled

¼ cup chopped fresh parsley

½ teaspoon salt

½ teaspoon sugar

1 tablespoon olive oil (optional, for flavor)

Freshly ground pepper to taste

1- In a large saucepan over medium heat, combine all ingredients. Stir well, bring to a simmer, cover and simmer, stirring occasionally to break up tomatoes, about 1 hour. Uncover and simmer until sauce thickens, about 25 minutes longer.

2- Use immediately or transfer to containers with tight-fitting lids and refrigerate up to 1 week or freeze up to 1 year.

MAKES ABOUT **4** CUPS.

Note: To peel tomatoes, drop in boiling water to cover for 20 seconds.

Note: For a smoother sauce, purée finished sauce in food processor or blender.

FRESH TOMATO SALSA

◦

Make this popular salsa several hours before serving, to allow the flavors to blend. Serve at room temperature with tortilla chips, in dips, or with grilled fish, chicken, or polenta.

4 tomatoes, seeded, chopped, and drained

½ cup diced green bell pepper (optional)

½ cup chopped yellow onion

1 tablespoon minced, seeded fresh jalapeño pepper
   (see note), or 1 tablespoon diced canned chilies

2 cloves garlic, minced

Juice of 1 small lime

1 tablespoon olive oil

¼ cup chopped fresh cilantro or parsley

1 tablespoon chopped fresh oregano, or
   ¾ teaspoon dried oregano, crumbled

½ teaspoon salt

Freshly ground pepper to taste

1- In a bowl stir together all ingredients. Cover and let stand at room temperature at least 1 hour, then store in refrigerator up to 3 days. Drain, if necessary, before using.

MAKES ABOUT *3* CUPS.

Note: When handling chilies, wear rubber gloves or hold the chilies under water to protect against oils that may cause burning to the skin. Keep fingers away from face and eyes. Wash hands with soapy water immediately afterward.

CHEESE-STUFFED ZUCCHINI

○

If you're tired of plain zucchini, try this cheese-laced version.

3 large zucchini, cut in half crosswise
1½ cups grated Monterey Jack cheese
¾ cup small curd cottage cheese
2 tablespoons freshly grated Parmesan cheese
1 tablespoon chopped fresh parsley
2 tablespoons fine dried bread crumbs
Paprika, for topping

1- Preheat oven to 350°F. In a saucepan combine zucchini with salted water to cover generously. Bring to a boil, reduce heat to low, cover, and simmer until partially cooked, about 7 minutes. Drain and immerse in cold water to cool; drain again. Cut zucchini halves in half lengthwise. Using a small spoon scoop out seeds and a small amount of pulp and discard or save for another use. Place zucchini, cut sides down, on paper towels to drain for a few minutes.

2- In a bowl combine cheeses, parsley, and crumbs and stir to mix well. Arrange zucchini pieces, hollow side up, in an oiled baking dish. Fill each piece with an equal amount of cheese mixture. Sprinkle with paprika. Bake, uncovered, until zucchini are tender and cheese is melted, about 20 minutes. Serve immediately.

SERVES *6*.

GREAT "GRATE" ZUCCHINI

○

The texture of grated zucchini mixed with sour cream makes a creative and appealing vegetable dish. Serve with Chicken with Honey-Mustard Glaze (page 107).

3 zucchini, unpeeled, grated

2 tablespoons butter or margarine,
    cut into bits

¼ to ⅓ cup light sour cream

¼ teaspoon salt

Freshly ground pepper to taste

Freshly grated Parmesan cheese,
    for topping

1- Preheat oven to 350°F. Place grated zucchini in an oiled 8-inch square baking dish. Blot zucchini with paper towel. Dot with butter.

2- Bake, uncovered, for 15 minutes. Pour off any liquid that has collected in bottom of dish. Stir in sour cream, salt, and pepper. Sprinkle with Parmesan cheese and bake until zucchini is tender and cheese melts, about 5 minutes longer. Serve immediately.

SERVES *4*.

VEGETABLE SAUTÉ

o

A variety of winter vegetables quickly prepared on the stove top and served tender-crisp.

> 4 cups water
> ¼ teaspoon salt, plus salt to taste
> 2 cups cauliflower florets
> 2 cups broccoli florets
> 1 to 2 tablespoons butter or margarine
> 1 tablespoon vegetable oil
> 1 cup chopped yellow onion
> ½ red bell pepper, seeded and chopped
> ½ pound fresh mushrooms, sliced
> 1 small zucchini, sliced
> 1 tablespoon red wine vinegar (optional)
> Salt and freshly ground pepper to taste
> Freshly grated Parmesan cheese, for topping

1- In a large saucepan bring water to a boil. Add salt and cauliflower and boil 2 minutes. Add broccoli and boil 5 minutes longer. Drain and cool under cold water; drain again and set aside.

2- In a large skillet over medium heat, melt 1 tablespoon butter with oil. Add onion and bell pepper and sauté 2 minutes. Add mushrooms and zucchini and sauté, stirring frequently, 3 minutes longer. Add more butter if needed to prevent sticking. Add cauliflower, broccoli, vinegar, salt, and pepper. Cook, stirring, until vegetables are tender-crisp, about 5 minutes. Transfer to a serving bowl and sprinkle with Parmesan cheese. Serve immediately.

SERVES *4* TO *6*.

STEAMED MIXED VEGETABLES
o

Native to Mexico, jicama (hee-ka-mah) is a tropical plant with edible roots. It is often served raw as an appetizer, but it is also delicious steamed. The addition of jicama to this dish adds texture and crunchiness.

> 1 small jicama, peeled and cut into
> ½-inch-wide strips
>
> 4 carrots, peeled and cut into
> ½-inch-wide strips
>
> 1 yellow onion, sliced
>
> 1 red bell pepper, seeded and cut into ½-inch-wide strips
>
> 1 zucchini, cut into
> ½-inch-wide strips
>
> 10 large fresh mushrooms, quartered
>
> ½ teaspoon dried dill
>
> ½ teaspoon salt
>
> ¼ teaspoon pepper
>
> 3 tablespoons butter or margarine

1- Place jicama, carrots, and onion on steamer rack over gently boiling water, cover, and steam 10 minutes. Add red pepper, zucchini, and mushrooms to steamer rack. Re-cover and steam until all vegetables are tender-crisp, about 10 minutes longer.

2- Transfer vegetables to a warmed serving bowl. Add dill, salt, pepper, and butter and toss well. Serve immediately.

SERVES **6**.

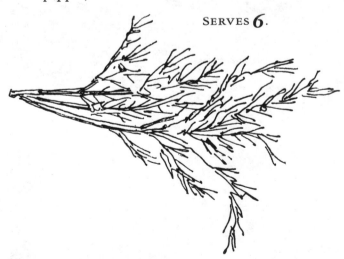

PASTA PLUS

○

Pasta—noodles, spaghetti, and macaroni—has long been popular on the West Coast, but not to the extent that it is today. Now, literally everyone seems to enjoy eating pasta. The reasons for its appeal are many. It is a high-energy food, inexpensive, and quick and easy to prepare. Served hot or cold with various combinations of vegetables, meats, seafood, and dairy products, pasta makes a satisfying meal on its own.

Fresh pasta can be made at home or found in the refrigerated section of supermarkets or at specialty pasta shops. It is perishable and must be well wrapped and stored in the refrigerator up to 5 days. Frozen pasta will keep up to 3 months. When cooking frozen pasta, do not thaw. Dried pasta comes packaged or in bulk in a wide assortment of sizes and shapes. Uses differ between these two pastas as well: Fresh pasta lends itself best to hot, delicate sauces, while dried pasta is better suited to cold pasta salads and more rustic sauces.

The proper cooking and serving of pasta is critical to its success.

PASTA BASICS

How much pasta to cook? The rule of thumb is 1 pound of pasta serves 8 for a side dish or first course and 4 for a main course. You may adjust these amounts, depending upon your menus and the appetites you are serving.

—

Cook pasta in a large pan in a generous amount of boiling water. Adding salt to the water is a personal choice. Allow 4 quarts of water for each pound of pasta. The pan must be large enough to permit the strands to roll around freely and cook evenly. Add pasta to boiling water and stir occasionally. Keep the water at a rolling boil throughout the cooking and do not cover the pan.

—

Do not overcook the pasta. Fresh pasta cooks in 1 to 2 minutes. Dried pasta takes longer; follow the package directions for the timing as shapes and sizes vary. To test for doneness, remove a strand and taste it. It should be firm to the bite—al dente—and a little chewy. Drain immediately; do not rinse the pasta under water unless it is to be used in a cold dish. At this point, the pasta can be returned to the pan and tossed with the sauce or other ingredients.

—

Serve the pasta immediately. Pasta must be piping hot to be good. Place it on a warmed serving dish or on warmed individual plates.

To store leftover pasta, mix with a little oil, cover, and refrigerate. To reheat pasta, drop into boiling water and stir gently for about 1 minute.

—

While the pasta market was booming, rice was being ignored. Now, however, it is coming back into its own, with a host of new variations. I have included some of these dishes here, along with some other wholesome grain and legume dishes. All of these foods are rich in fiber and should be included regularly in the daily diet.

RICE BASICS

Follow cooking directions on the package, as each type of rice requires different measurements and timing. For a more flavorful rice, substitute broth for water.

—

Generally, simmer rice, covered, until liquid is absorbed. Do not uncover during cooking time and do not stir.

—

Prepare rice just before serving time. Fluff the kernels with a fork before serving.

—

One cup uncooked long-grain rice will yield 3 cups cooked rice and will serve 4.

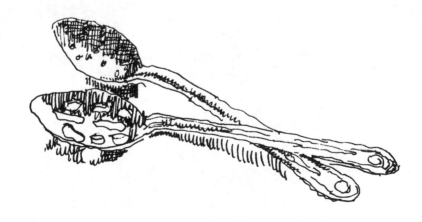

FETTUCCINE ALFREDO
WITH SPINACH
○

Treat your guests (and yourself) to one of the most favored of all pastas. This rich, creamy pasta with spinach is good served with seafood.

2 bunches spinach, about ½ pound each

1 cup half-and-half

6 tablespoons butter

¼ teaspoon white pepper

1 cup freshly grated Parmesan cheese

¼ teaspoon salt

¾ pound fresh fettuccine, cooked and drained

1- In a large covered skillet over high heat, cook spinach, with a little water until wilted, about 2 minutes. Toss with a fork once or twice while cooking. Drain well, chop, and set aside.

2- In the same skillet over medium heat, combine half-and-half, butter, and pepper. When butter is melted, stir in cheese and salt. Reduce heat to low and continue cooking, stirring occasionally, until cheese is melted and sauce is slightly thickened, about 5 minutes. Do not boil.

3- Add fettuccine and spinach and toss well. Transfer to a warmed serving dish and serve immediately.

SERVES *4* AS A SIDE DISH.

VARIATION:

Add 1 cup small cooked shrimp or chopped chicken (preferably white meat) with the half-and-half.

GARDEN PASTA

o

Most pasta dishes should be assembled just before serving. Have all the ingredients and equipment ready before you start to cook, so the dish will go together smoothly.

4 or 5 tablespoons butter or margarine

2 tablespoons vegetable oil

1 small yellow onion, chopped

1 clove garlic, minced

½ red bell pepper, seeded and chopped

1 large zucchini, halved lengthwise
and then cut into ¼-inch-thick slices

¾ pound fresh mushrooms, quartered

1 tablespoon chopped fresh basil, or
¾ teaspoon dried basil, crumbled

¼ teaspoon dried marjoram, crumbled

½ teaspoon salt

⅛ teaspoon pepper

2 tablespoons fresh lemon juice

¼ cup freshly grated Parmesan cheese,
plus additional cheese for serving (optional)

12 ounces fresh fettuccine, cooked and drained

1- In a large skillet over medium heat, melt 2 tablespoons of the butter with oil. Add onion, garlic, and bell pepper and sauté 3 minutes. Add zucchini, mushrooms, basil, marjoram, salt, and pepper. Sauté, stirring occasionally, 5 minutes longer. Add lemon juice, cover, and cook until vegetables are tender, about 5 minutes.

2- Add to skillet remaining 2 or 3 tablespoons butter, ¼ cup cheese, and fettuccine and toss gently. Serve immediately in a warmed serving dish or on warmed individual plates. Pass additional Parmesan cheese, if desired.

SERVES **6** AS A SIDE DISH.

Note: If pasta seems dry after tossing with sauce, cheese, and remaining butter, add 1 to 2 more tablespoons butter or margarine and toss well.

Pasta with Broccoli and Tomato

○

A delicious pasta dish that goes together fast when you haven't much time to cook.

¼ teaspoon salt

3 cups coarsely chopped broccoli florets

2 tablespoons vegetable oil

1 cup chopped yellow onion

½ red bell pepper, seeded and chopped

2 cloves garlic, minced

1 tomato, seeded and chopped

½ teaspoon salt

¼ teaspoon red pepper flakes

8 ounces dried fusilli, cooked and drained

Freshly ground pepper to taste

½ cup freshly grated Parmesan cheese,
   plus additional cheese for serving (optional)

2 tablespoons butter or margarine

¼ cup chopped fresh parsley

1- Fill a large saucepan with water and bring to a boil. Add salt and broccoli and boil 3 minutes. Drain and immerse in cold water to cool completely; drain again and set aside.

2- In a large skillet over medium heat, warm oil. Add onion, bell pepper, and garlic and sauté 4 minutes. Add tomato, salt, pepper flakes, and reserved broccoli and sauté, stirring occasionally, until vegetables are heated through, about 3 minutes.

3- Add pasta, pepper, cheese, butter, and parsley and toss gently. Serve immediately in a warmed serving dish or on warmed individual plates. Pass more Parmesan cheese, if desired.

SERVES *4* AS A SIDE DISH.

VERMICELLI WITH BASIL PESTO
○

The pesto clings to the pasta, making a pretty green side dish. This is excellent with chicken or fish.

½ pound dried vermicelli, cooked and drained

½ cup Basil Pesto (recipe follows), at room temperature

Salt and freshly ground pepper to taste

1 tomato, seeded, diced, and drained

1- Place drained pasta in a warmed serving bowl. Add pesto and toss gently. Season with salt and pepper and top with tomatoes. Serve immediately.

SERVES **4** AS A SIDE DISH.

BASIL PESTO
○

2 cups firmly packed fresh basil leaves

1 cup firmly packed fresh parsley sprigs

¼ cup freshly grated Parmesan cheese

2 tablespoons pine nuts or chopped walnuts

2 large cloves garlic, halved

⅓ to ½ cup olive oil

1- In food processor or blender, combine basil, parsley, cheese, nuts, and garlic. Process until herbs are finely chopped. With motor running, slowly add oil. Scrape down sides of container several times and continue to process until a smooth, creamy sauce forms. Place in a covered container and refrigerate. This also freezes well for up to 4 months.

MAKES ABOUT **1** CUP.

Note: Pesto may turn dark on top. This is normal.

GOLDEN PILAF
o

An easy pasta-rice dish to accompany grilled meats.

¼ cup butter
½ cup broken (½-inch lengths) dried vermicelli
1 cup long-grain white rice
2 cups chicken broth

1- In a saucepan over medium heat, melt butter. Add vermicelli and sauté until golden, about 4 minutes. Add rice and stir until kernels are coated. Add broth, cover, and cook over low heat until liquid is absorbed, about 20 minutes.

2- Serve immediately.

SERVES *6* AS A SIDE DISH.

CHEESE MANICOTTI
o

When some family members became vegetarians a few years ago, this was one of their favorite dishes. No eggs, no meat, but a creamy filling and savory tomato sauce.

FILLING:

    3 ounces cream cheese, at room temperature

    1 cup grated mozzarella cheese

    2 cups small curd cottage cheese or ricotta cheese

    3 tablespoons freshly grated Parmesan cheese

    ¼ teaspoon salt

    ¼ cup chopped fresh parsley

    2 cups Fresh Tomato Sauce (page 234) or
      Quick Tomato Sauce (page 251)

    12 dried manicotti shells, cooked,
      well drained, and cooled slightly

    ¼ to ½ cup freshly grated Parmesan cheese,
      for topping

    1 cup grated mozzarella cheese, for topping

1- To make filling, in a bowl combine all ingredients and mix well.

2- Preheat oven to 350°F. Pour ½ cup tomato sauce into an oiled 9-by-13-inch baking dish. Using a spoon, fill manicotti shells with filling. Place filled shells in a single layer in prepared dish. Pour remaining tomato sauce over top.

3- Cover and bake 20 minutes. Uncover and sprinkle with Parmesan and mozzarella cheeses. Bake, uncovered, until bubbly, about 15 minutes longer. Let stand 10 minutes before serving.

SERVES *6* TO *8* AS A MAIN DISH.

Note: If you wish to freeze half the recipe, before baking, divide it between 2 dishes. Cover dish tightly with aluminum foil before freezing.

Pasta with Chicken, Zucchini, Mushrooms, and Tomato Sauce

○

A main dish pasta with chicken and vegetables that is healthful and satisfying. Serve with a mixed green salad and crusty bread.

> 1 large zucchini, halved lengthwise and
>   cut into ¼-inch-thick slices
>
> 4 large fresh mushrooms, quartered
>
> 1½ cups cubed, cooked chicken breast
>
> 2 cups Fresh Tomato Sauce (page 234) or
>   Quick Tomato Sauce (recipe follows)
>
> 8 ounces (2½ cups) penne or mostaccioli,
>   cooked and drained
>
> Salt and freshly ground pepper to taste
>
> Freshly grated Parmesan cheese,
>   for topping

1- Place zucchini and mushrooms on a steamer rack over gently boiling water, cover, and steam until tender-crisp, about 6 minutes.

2- Remove rack and pour off water. In same pan combine zucchini, mushrooms, chicken, and tomato sauce. Simmer to blend flavors, about 5 minutes. Add drained pasta, salt, and pepper and toss gently to mix well.

3- Transfer to a warmed bowl, sprinkle with Parmesan cheese, and serve immediately.

SERVES *4*.

QUICK TOMATO SAUCE

○

This all-purpose tomato sauce can be used with pastas, meats, and fish.

1 tablespoon olive oil or vegetable oil

1 cup chopped yellow onion

1 large clove garlic, minced

1 can (16 ounces) plum tomatoes,
    coarsely chopped, with juices

1 can (8 ounces) tomato sauce

½ teaspoon dried basil, crumbled

¼ teaspoon dried oregano, crumbled

1 bay leaf

¼ teaspoon sugar

¼ teaspoon salt

Freshly ground pepper to taste

1- In a saucepan over medium heat, warm oil. Add onion and garlic and sauté until soft, about 5 minutes. Meanwhile, purée tomatoes and juices slightly in food processor. Add with tomato sauce, herbs, sugar, salt, and pepper to pan. Simmer, uncovered, stirring occasionally, until slightly thickened and flavors are blended, 10 to 15 minutes.

2- Remove bay leaf and discard. Serve immediately or cover and refrigerate up to 1 week.

MAKES ABOUT *3* CUPS.

Note: For a smoother sauce, purée finished sauce in food processor or blender.

ORZO, SPINACH, AND MUSHROOMS

○

Orzo is a small oval pasta that looks like rice kernels but has its own distinctive texture and flavor. Cooked with spinach and mushrooms, it makes a delightful side dish.

3 cups chicken broth or water

¼ teaspoon salt

1 cup orzo

3 tablespoons butter or margarine

½ cup chopped yellow onion

½ pound fresh mushrooms, sliced

2 cloves garlic, minced

1 bunch spinach, about ½ pound, chopped

1 to 2 tablespoons water

½ cup freshly grated Parmesan cheese

Dash of ground nutmeg

Salt and pepper to taste

1- In a saucepan over high heat, bring broth and salt to a boil. Add orzo and stir well. Reduce heat to medium-low or low, cover, and cook until tender, 15 to 20 minutes. Drain off any liquid that remains and set orzo aside.

2- In a large skillet with a lid over medium heat, melt butter. Add onion and sauté 2 minutes. Add mushrooms and garlic and sauté, stirring frequently, 3 to 4 minutes longer. Remove onion, mushrooms, and garlic to a bowl.

3- Add spinach and water to skillet. Cover and cook, turning once or twice with a fork, until spinach wilts, about 2 minutes. Drain if necessary and return onion and mushrooms to skillet along with orzo. Add cheese, nutmeg, salt, and pepper, toss to mix well, and heat through. Transfer to a warmed serving dish and serve immediately.

SERVES *6* AS A SIDE DISH.

FRESH CORN POLENTA

○

Polenta is essentially the same cornmeal mush my mother used to fry and serve with syrup for breakfast. Although polenta is Italian, this version, with fresh corn, cheese, and chilies, makes a delicious side dish that complements Mexican food. Serve with Black Bean Salsa (page 189), Fresh Tomato Salsa (page 235), and sour cream.

¼ cup butter or margarine, melted

2 eggs, beaten

½ cup grated Monterey Jack cheese

½ cup grated Cheddar cheese

2 cups fresh corn kernels (from about 4 ears),
    or 1 package (10 ounces) frozen corn,
    thawed and well drained

½ cup yellow cornmeal

1 cup sour cream

1 tablespoon sugar

1 teaspoon salt

1 can (4 ounces) diced green chilies, drained

¼ cup freshly grated Parmesan cheese

1- Preheat oven to 350°F. In a bowl mix together all ingredients except Parmesan cheese. Place in an oiled 7½-by-11¼-inch baking dish.

2- Bake, uncovered until firm, 40 minutes. Sprinkle with Parmesan cheese and bake 5 minutes longer.

SERVES **6** AS A SIDE DISH.

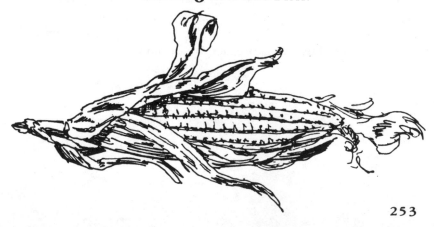

POLENTA WITH
FRESH TOMATO SAUCE
○

*Serve this polenta dish with tomato sauce and hot Italian sausage.
Chicken broth gives the polenta a richer flavor.*

2½ cups chicken broth

1 teaspoon salt

1¼ cups cornmeal

1 cup water

3 tablespoons freshly grated Parmesan cheese

1 tablespoon butter or margarine

1 cup Fresh Tomato Sauce (page 234) or
  Quick Tomato Sauce (page 251), heated

1- In a saucepan bring broth and salt to a boil. Meanwhile, in a
pitcher stir together cornmeal and water.

2- Slowly add cornmeal mixture to boiling broth, stirring constantly. Cook over low heat, stirring often, until thickened, about
5 minutes. Stir in cheese and butter.

3- Serve immediately with tomato sauce.

SERVES *4* AS A SIDE DISH.

VARIATION:

To make grilled or fried polenta, pour cooked polenta into an oiled
8-inch square baking dish, cover, and refrigerate until well chilled
and firm. Cut chilled polenta into 2-inch squares. Grill squares
on oiled grill rack or fry in 1 to 2 tablespoons butter over medium
heat, turning once, until lightly browned and crispy, about 4 minutes. Serve with Fresh Tomato Sauce. Also good with syrup or honey
for breakfast.

BARLEY-RICE-NUT PILAF

o

This chewy, nutty side dish goes well with roast chicken or pork chops.

¼ cup butter or margarine

¼ cup slivered almonds or pine nuts

1 cup chopped yellow onion

1 clove garlic, minced

⅔ cup long-grain brown rice

⅓ cup pearl barley

2 cups chicken broth

¼ cup dry white wine

1 tablespoon chopped fresh basil, or
    ¾ teaspoon dried basil, crumbled

1 teaspoon chopped fresh oregano, or
    ½ teaspoon dried oregano, crumbled

¼ teaspoon salt

Freshly ground pepper

¼ cup chopped fresh parsley

1- Preheat oven to 350°F. In a saucepan over medium heat melt butter. Add nuts and sauté, stirring constantly, until lightly browned, about 2 minutes. Add onion and garlic and sauté until soft, about 5 minutes. Stir in rice and barley, and then add broth, wine, basil, oregano, salt, pepper, and parsley. Place in an oiled 2-quart baking dish.

2- Cover and bake until liquid is absorbed and rice and barley are tender, about 1 hour. Serve immediately.

SERVES *6* AS A SIDE DISH.

Black Beans with Sour Cream and Chopped Tomatoes

○

A popular side dish that goes well with Chicken with Chiles and Cheese (page 104) or other Mexican menus.

> 2 cups dried black beans
>
> 6 cups water
>
> 1 bay leaf
>
> ¼ teaspoon ground cumin
>
> ¼ teaspoon dried oregano, crumbled
>
> Salt and black pepper, to taste
>
> ⅛ teaspoon cayenne pepper
>
> Sour cream or plain nonfat yogurt, for topping
>
> 2 hard-cooked eggs, chopped, for topping
>
> 1 small tomato, seeded and chopped, for topping

1- Rinse and sort beans and place in a large saucepan. Add the water and bring to a boil. Boil for 2 minutes. Turn off heat, cover, and let stand 1 hour.

2- Add bay leaf to beans and return to a boil. Cover, reduce heat to low, and simmer until beans are tender, about 1½ hours.

3- Drain off all but 1 cup of liquid from beans. Remove bay leaf and discard. Add cumin, oregano, salt, and black and cayenne peppers and simmer, uncovered, 20 minutes. (Beans may be prepared up to this point, covered, and refrigerated until serving time, then reheated to serving temperature.)

4- Drain beans, if necessary, and place in serving bowl. Top with sour cream or yogurt, egg, and chopped tomatoes. Serve immediately.

SERVES **6** AS MAIN COURSE, **10** TO **12** AS A SIDE DISH.

HAZELNUT-RICE CASSEROLE
o

An easy-to-make side dish for grilled meats or chicken. The hazelnuts add extra crunch and flavor.

1 cup long-grain brown rice

1 cup water

1 cup chicken or beef broth

1 tablespoon soy sauce

2 teaspoons Worcestershire sauce

¼ teaspoon salt

⅛ teaspoon pepper

¼ cup chopped, toasted hazelnuts
  (see note, page 64)

2 tablespoons butter or margarine, cut up

1- Preheat oven to 350°F. In a bowl stir together all ingredients. Place in an oiled 2-quart baking dish.

2- Cover and bake until liquid is absorbed and rice is tender, about 1 hour. Serve immediately.

SERVES **6** AS A SIDE DISH.

RICE AND WHEAT BERRY PILAF
o

Here is a recipe for cooks looking for something a little different to add to their menus. Wheat berries (whole unprocessed wheat kernels) add a pleasant nutty flavor and chewy texture. The berries must be soaked in water at least 6 hours or as long as overnight before using.

2 tablespoons butter or margarine

4 large shallots, about 3 ounces total weight,
    finely chopped

½ cup wheat berries, soaked in water to cover
    from 6 hours to overnight and then drained

⅔ cup long-grain brown rice

2 cups chicken broth

½ teaspoon salt

¼ teaspoon dried oregano, crumbled

3 tablespoons chopped fresh parsley

½ cup chopped walnuts

1- In a saucepan over medium heat, melt butter. Add shallots and sauté until soft, about 4 minutes. Add wheat berries and rice and stir well. Add broth, salt, oregano, and parsley. Bring to a boil, reduce heat to low, cover, and cook until rice and wheat berries are tender and liquid is absorbed, 40 to 45 minutes.

2- Stir in nuts and serve immediately.

SERVES *8* AS A SIDE DISH.

SPICY PEACH PILAF
o

This sweet, spicy rice dish complements pork or lamb. Canned peaches can be used if fresh peaches are not in season.

2 cups water

½ teaspoon salt

1 cup long-grain white rice

¼ teaspoon ground cinnamon

¼ teaspoon ground ginger

¼ teaspoon ground nutmeg

⅛ teaspoon ground cloves

1 tablespoon honey

2 tablespoons butter or margarine

2 large peaches, peeled, pitted, and
    cut into bite-size pieces

¼ cup slivered blanched almonds,
    toasted (see note, page 63)

1- In a saucepan bring water and salt to a boil. Add rice, cover, reduce heat to low, and cook until liquid is absorbed, about 20 minutes.

2- Add spices, honey, butter, peaches, and nuts. Mix well and heat over medium-low heat until flavors are blended and peaches are warm, about 3 minutes. Serve immediately.

SERVES *6* AS A SIDE DISH.

Note: To peel peaches, drop into boiling water 10 to 20 seconds, drain, and then slip off skins. Apricots can be peeled in the same way.

SPINACH-RICE CASSEROLE

○

This recipe is adapted from a dish served in an old San Francisco restaurant. It has become a family favorite and a traditional accompaniment to barbecued turkey or salmon.

> 2 bunches fresh spinach, about ½ pound each,
>   or 2 packages (10 ounces each) frozen chopped
>   spinach, thawed and squeezed dry
>
> 3 eggs
>
> ⅔ cup milk
>
> 2 tablespoons butter or margarine, melted
>
> ½ cup finely chopped yellow onion
>
> 2 tablespoons chopped fresh parsley
>
> 1 teaspoon dried thyme, crumbled
>
> 1 teaspoon salt
>
> ¼ teaspoon ground nutmeg
>
> 1 teaspoon Worcestershire sauce
>
> 3 cups cooked long-grain brown or white rice (1 cup raw)
>
> 3 cups grated sharp Cheddar cheese

1- Preheat oven to 350°F. If using fresh spinach, cook with a small amount of water in a large covered saucepan over high heat until wilted, about 2 minutes. Toss with a fork once or twice while cooking. Drain well, pressing out excess water, chop, and set aside.

2- In a large bowl, using a whisk, beat eggs until blended. Add milk, butter, onion, parsley, thyme, salt, nutmeg, and Worcestershire sauce and mix well. Fold in rice, 2 cups of the cheese, and reserved spinach. Turn the mixture into an oiled 3-quart casserole or baking dish.

3- Bake, uncovered, until bubbling and golden, about 45 minutes. Remove from oven, sprinkle remaining 1 cup cheese evenly over top, and return to oven to melt, about 5 minutes longer. Serve immediately.

SERVES *8* AS A SIDE DISH.

MUSHROOM-LEEK-RICE PILAF
o

Leeks have a mild, sweet taste that adds depth and flavor to any dish. This is a perfect accompaniment for beef roast or steaks.

2 leeks, white part only

¼ cup butter or margarine

2 cups sliced fresh mushrooms
(about ⅓ pound)

1 cup long-grain white rice

2 cups chicken broth

1 tablespoon chopped fresh basil, or
¾ teaspoon dried basil, crumbled

¼ teaspoon dried thyme, crumbled

¼ teaspoon salt

⅛ teaspoon pepper

¼ cup chopped fresh parsley

1- Cut off root ends of leeks and split lengthwise. Rinse under running water, separating the leaves with your fingers to allow the sand to be flushed out. Slice thinly.

2- In a saucepan over medium heat, melt butter. Add leeks and mushrooms and sauté, stirring frequently, until vegetables are soft, about 6 minutes. Add rice and stir to coat kernels with butter. Add broth, basil, thyme, salt, and pepper. Bring to a boil, reduce heat to medium-low, cover, and simmer until liquid is absorbed, about 25 minutes.

3- Just before serving, stir in parsley. Transfer to a warmed bowl and serve immediately.

SERVES *4* TO *6* AS A SIDE DISH.

CURRIED LENTILS

○

For variety, serve this high-fiber lentil dish in place of rice or pasta.
It goes particularly well with roast lamb or pork. Lentils do not need
presoaking but they do need to be rinsed and sorted before cooking.

1 cup dried lentils, rinsed and sorted

1 clove garlic, minced

1 bay leaf

1½ cups chicken broth

¼ teaspoon salt

¼ teaspoon dried oregano, crumbled

¼ teaspoon curry powder

1 tablespoon butter or margarine (optional)

Freshly ground pepper to taste

1- In a saucepan combine lentils, garlic, bay leaf, and broth. Bring
to a boil, reduce heat to medium-low, cover, and simmer until
tender and liquid is absorbed, about 35 minutes.

2- Remove bay leaf and discard. Mix in salt, oregano, curry powder,
butter, and pepper. Serve immediately.

SERVES **4** AS A SIDE DISH.

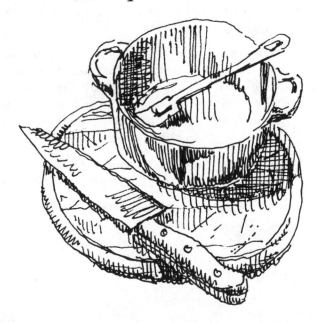

WALNUT AND BULGUR CASSEROLE

○

The walnuts and bulgur give a doubly nutty flavor to this casserole. It can be served hot or at room temperature. Serve with Cheddar Cheese Sauce, or with Dijon Chicken (page 119) and use the sauce on the bulgur.

1½ cups bulgur (cracked wheat)

1 cup water

1 tablespoon vegetable oil

1 cup chopped yellow onion

½ green bell pepper, seeded and chopped

1 cup chopped walnuts

1 tomato, seeded and chopped

2 eggs, lightly beaten

1 cup chicken broth

¼ cup chopped fresh parsley

½ teaspoon salt

½ teaspoon dried basil, crumbled

¼ teaspoon ground coriander

⅛ teaspoon pepper

Cheddar Cheese Sauce (recipe follows)

1- In a bowl large enough to hold all ingredients, mix together bulgur and water. Let stand 1 hour.

2- Preheat oven to 350°F. In a skillet over medium heat, warm oil. Add onion and bell pepper and sauté 3 minutes. Add walnuts and tomato and cook, stirring, until vegetables are soft, about 3 minutes. Add vegetable and walnut mixture to bowl containing bulgur. Add eggs, broth, parsley, salt, basil, coriander, and pepper and mix well. Transfer to an oiled 2-quart baking dish.

3- Cover and bake until bulgur is soft and well heated, about 30 minutes. Serve immediately or let cool and serve at room temperature.

SERVES *6* TO *8* AS A SIDE DISH.

CHEDDAR CHEESE SAUCE

o

This sauce is also good on broccoli or asparagus.

2 tablespoons butter or margarine
2 tablespoons all-purpose flour
¼ teaspoon salt
⅛ teaspoon cayenne pepper
¼ teaspoon paprika
1¼ cups milk
1 cup grated Cheddar cheese

1- In a saucepan over medium-high heat, melt butter. Stir in flour and cook, stirring, 1 minute. Season with salt, cayenne pepper, and paprika. Slowly stir in milk and cook, stirring constantly, until sauce bubbles and thickens, about 3 minutes. Add cheese and stir until it melts. Serve immediately.

MAKES ABOUT *1 1/2* CUPS.

SWEET TALK

○

The dessert is the "finishing touch" to a meal and is often the highlight of the dinner. It can be as elaborate or as simple as you wish, but it should always complement the rest of the meal.

Light, refreshing desserts are more popular now, with rich desserts being reserved for special occasions. Fruit desserts should be made when the fruit is at its seasonal peak and bursting with flavor.

The West Coast is well known for its production of fresh seasonal fruits, many of which are distributed nationally and internationally. A number of the desserts in this section showcase West Coast fruits, nuts, and berries. Others are a collection of family favorites.

FALL CREEK BLUEBERRY CRISP

○

We eat a lot of blueberries at our house because our son grows blueberry plants commercially in the small community of Fall Creek, Oregon. Among the most versatile of all the fruits, blueberries can be eaten at breakfast, lunch, or dinner and used to make sauces, breads, jams, cakes, pies, and crisps. They are also easy to use, since they require no peeling, seeding, coring, or chopping. Frozen blueberries retain their color, texture, and flavor, so load up the freezer for off-season enjoyment. This recipe goes together in just a few minutes with blueberries from the freezer.

> 2 pints (4 cups) fresh or thawed, frozen blueberries
> 1 tablespoon all-purpose flour
> ⅓ cup sugar
> Juice of 1 lemon
> TOPPING:
> ½ cup butter or margarine, at room temperature
> ½ cup sugar
> ¾ cup all-purpose flour
> Dash of salt
> Vanilla ice cream or frozen yogurt

1- Preheat oven to 350°F. Place blueberries in an oiled 8-inch square baking dish. Add flour, sugar, and lemon juice and mix well.

2- To make topping, in food processor combine all ingredients. Using off-on pulses, process until crumbly. Or combine ingredients in a bowl and, using a pastry blender, cut in butter until crumbly. Sprinkle topping over blueberry mixture.

3- Bake until berries are bubbly and top is lightly browned, about 35 minutes. Cool on a wire rack 15 minutes, then spoon into dishes and top with ice cream.

SERVES *6*.

FRESH PEACH-BLUEBERRY CRISP
o

This recipe combines contrasting colors and flavors for a delectable dessert. Top with vanilla ice cream or frozen yogurt.

> 5 large peaches, peeled, halved, and pitted, (see note)
> 1½ pints (3 cups) blueberries
>
> TOPPING:
>> ½ cup all-purpose flour
>> ½ cup old-fashioned rolled oats
>> ¾ cup firmly packed brown sugar
>> ½ cup butter or margarine, at room temperature
>> Vanilla ice cream or frozen yogurt

1- Preheat oven to 350°F. Place peach halves, cut side down, in a buttered 7 ½-by-11 ¾-inch glass baking dish. Spread blueberries evenly over top.

2- To make topping, in food processor combine all ingredients. Using off-on pulses, process until crumbly. Or combine ingredients in a bowl and, using a pastry blender, cut in butter until crumbly. Sprinkle topping evenly over fruits.

3- Bake until fruit is bubbly and topping is lightly browned, about 40 minutes. Cool on wire rack. Serve warm or at room temperature with ice cream.

SERVES *6* TO *8*.

Note: To peel peaches (and apricots), drop in boiling water for 15 to 20 seconds, drain, and then slip off skins.

VERY BERRY COBBLER

○

Watch for berries to appear in your market or produce stand and make this dessert treat when a good variety of fresh berries is at its peak. Any combination of berries can be used with good results.

¼ cup butter or margarine, at room temperature

1 cup sugar

1 cup all-purpose flour

2 tablespoons baking powder

¼ teaspoon salt

½ cup milk

2 pints (4 cups) mixed berries such as raspberries, marionberries, boysenberries, blueberries, or blackberries

1 cup boiling water

Vanilla ice cream or frozen yogurt

1- Preheat oven to 350°F. In a bowl and using an electric mixer, cream together butter and ½ of the cup sugar until fluffy. In another bowl or on a large sheet of waxed paper, combine flour, baking powder, and salt. One third at a time and beating well after each addition, add dry ingredients alternately with milk to butter-sugar mixture. Beat until smooth.

2- Spoon batter into an oiled 2-quart baking dish. Distribute berries evenly over batter. Sprinkle on the remaining ½ cup sugar and then pour the boiling water evenly over the berries.

3- Bake until top is golden and the juices are bubbling, 40 to 45 minutes. Cool on wire rack. Serve warm or at room temperature with ice cream.

SERVES *6*.

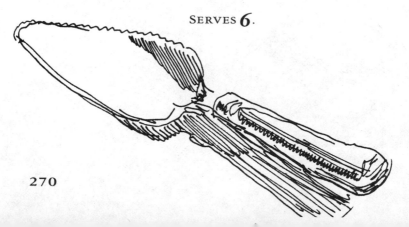

CRAN-APPLE CRISP

○

Freeze cranberries when they are in season so you can make this crisp anytime of the year. The sweet, tart flavor is just right after a big meal. It is a good change from the usual pumpkin dessert for Thanksgiving dinner.

2 cups fresh or frozen cranberries

4 green apples, peeled, cored, and sliced

¾ cup sugar

1 tablespoon fresh lemon juice

Dash of salt

TOPPING:

½ cup all-purpose flour

1 cup old-fashioned rolled oats

¾ cup firmly packed brown sugar

¼ teaspoon ground cinnamon

Dash of ground nutmeg

¼ teaspoon salt

½ cup butter or margarine, at room temperature

¼ cup chopped walnuts or toasted hazelnuts
(see note, page 64)

1- Preheat oven to 350°F. In a bowl combine cranberries, apples, sugar, lemon juice, and salt. Mix well. Transfer to an oiled 9-by-13-inch baking dish.

2- To make topping, in food processor combine flour, oats, sugar, spices, salt, and butter. Using off-on pulses, process until crumbly. Or combine ingredients in a bowl and, using a pastry blender, cut in butter until crumbly. Mix in nuts. Sprinkle topping over fruit mixture.

3- Bake until fruit is juicy and topping is lightly browned, about 40 minutes. Cool on wire rack. Serve warm or at room temperature.

SERVES *6* TO *8*.

APPLE CRUMB PIE
o

The Northwest, especially Washington State, boasts about its apple production. Washington apples are shipped all over the world and are famous for their brilliant color, bright flavor, and crisp texture. I like to put this scrumptious pie in the oven just before dinner so it can be served warm. Topping it with vanilla ice cream or frozen yogurt makes it even better. Serve with a wedge of sharp Cheddar cheese.

> 9-inch unbaked pie shell made from
> No-Fail Pie Pastry (recipe follows)
>
> 6 Golden Delicious apples or any good
> cooking apples, peeled, cored, and sliced
>
> 1 tablespoon fresh lemon juice
>
> Dash of salt
>
> ½ cup granulated sugar
>
> 1 teaspoon ground cinnamon
>
> ½ cup firmly packed brown sugar
>
> ¾ cup all-purpose flour
>
> 6 tablespoons butter or margarine,
> at room temperature
>
> Vanilla ice cream or frozen yogurt,
> for topping
>
> Cheddar cheese wedges (optional)

1- Preheat oven to 400°F. Prepare pie shell.

2- In a bowl combine apples, lemon juice, salt, granulated sugar, and cinnamon and mix well. Place in pie shell.

3- In a small bowl combine brown sugar, flour, and butter. Using a pastry blender, cut in butter until crumbly. Sprinkle evenly over apples.

4- Bake 20 minutes. Reduce oven temperature to 350°F and bake until top is golden and filling is bubbling, 25 to 30 minutes longer. Cool on wire rack. Serve warm or at room temperature with ice cream and with Cheddar cheese, if desired.

SERVES *6* TO *8*.

NO-FAIL PIE PASTRY
o

If you have trouble with pastry, this is a no-fail recipe. This method has become popular lately because it uses vegetable oil instead of shortening.

> 1⅓ cups all-purpose flour
>
> ½ teaspoon salt
>
> ⅓ cup vegetable oil
>
> 2 tablespoons cold water

1- In a bowl stir together flour, salt, and oil until flour is moistened. Slowly add water, 1 tablespoon at a time, tossing with a fork until water is incorporated. Pat dough into a ball.

2- Place dough in a 9-inch glass pie plate. Using your fingers press out dough evenly onto bottom and up sides of plate. Continue pressing until dough covers the plate edge and then flute the edge. Fill unbaked shell with filling.

Note: For a prebaked shell, to hold a cooked filling, prick the bottom and sides of unbaked shell thoroughly with a fork. Bake in preheated 475°F oven until golden, about 10 minutes. Cool thoroughly on wire rack before filling.

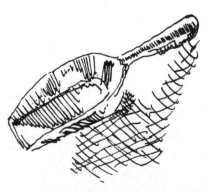

273

RHUBARB-STRAWBERRY CRUMBLE
O

This recipe combines the tart flavor of rhubarb and the sweet flavor of strawberries with a crunchy oatmeal-nut topping.

>   4 cups sliced (1-inch pieces) rhubarb
>   (about 2 pounds)
>   1 pint (2 cups) strawberries, hulled and sliced
>   1 cup sugar
>   ¼ cup fresh orange juice
> TOPPING:
>   1 cup all-purpose flour
>   ½ teaspoon ground cinnamon
>   ⅛ teaspoon salt
>   ½ cup butter or margarine, at
>   room temperature, cut up
>   ½ cup old-fashioned rolled oats
>   ½ cup walnuts pieces
>   Vanilla ice cream or frozen yogurt

1- Preheat oven to 350°F. In an oiled 7 ½-by-11 ¾-inch square baking dish, combine rhubarb, strawberries, sugar, and juice. Stir to mix well.

2- To make topping, in food processor combine all ingredients. Using off-on pulses, process until crumbly. Or combine ingredients in a bowl and, using a pastry blender, cut in butter until crumbly. Sprinkle topping evenly over rhubarb and strawberries.

3- Bake until top is golden and juices are bubbling, about 45 minutes. Cool on wire rack. Serve warm or at room temperature with ice cream.

SERVES *6*.

PEACH GLAZE PIE
o

Summer's juicy, ripe peaches in a graham cracker–nut crust make a perfect ending for a patio party.

> 5 large peaches, peeled, pitted, and sliced
> (see note page 269)
>
> ½ cup sugar
>
> 2 tablespoons cornstarch
>
> 3 tablespoons water
>
> 9-inch prebaked Graham Cracker–Nut Crust
> (recipe follows)
>
> Vanilla ice cream or whipped cream, for topping

1- In food processor or blender process 1½ cups peach slices to make about 1 cup purée. Transfer to a saucepan and add sugar. In a small bowl mix cornstarch with water and add to pan. Cook over medium-high heat, stirring constantly, until mixture bubbles and thickens, about 3 minutes. Set aside to cool 5 minutes.

2- Stir remaining peach slices into purée mixture and pour into baked crust. Chill several hours in the refrigerator before serving. Serve with ice cream.

SERVES 6.

GRAHAM CRACKER–NUT CRUST
o

> 20 squares graham crackers
>
> 3 tablespoons slivered blanched almonds
>
> ⅓ cup butter or margarine, melted
>
> 3 tablespoons sugar

1- Preheat oven to 350°F. In food processor combine graham crackers and nuts and process to make about 1½ cups crumbs. In a bowl combine crumbs with butter and sugar. Transfer mixture to a 9-inch glass pie plate. With fingers, press crumb mixture firmly on bottom and up sides of plate.

2- Bake until crust is set, about 8 minutes. Cool on wire rack before adding the filling.

BEST STRAWBERRY PIE

○

A favorite aunt of mine traditionally made this pie for our family reunions. In fact, she always brought two strawberry pies because they were the first dessert to go. Strawberries are available from Southern California and Mexico in the early spring and from the Northwest in late spring and early summer.

> 9-inch prebaked pie shell made from
>   No-Fail Pie Pastry (page 273)
> 2 pints (4 cups) strawberries, hulled
> 1 cup sugar
> ¼ cup water
> 3 tablespoons cornstarch
> 1 cup whipping cream, whipped

1- Prepare and bake pie shell and let cool completely.

2- Cover bottom of pie shell with the largest berries in a single layer.

3- In a saucepan mash the remaining berries, then mix in sugar. In a small bowl stir together water and cornstarch. Heat mashed berries over medium heat and stir in cornstarch mixture. Continue to stir until thickened and mixture is clear, about 5 minutes. Remove from heat and let cool slightly.

4- Pour cooled berry mixture over whole berries. Cover and refrigerate until chilled. Serve with whipped cream.

SERVES 6.

CRANBERRY FLAMBÉ
○

An elegant dessert with a lot of flair, especially if you have a flambé pan to bring to the table. It makes a grand finale to a gourmet dinner.

½ cup honey

¼ cup water

1 tablespoon Curaçao (orange-flavored) liqueur

½ teaspoon grated orange zest

½ teaspoon grated lemon zest

3 cups fresh or frozen cranberries

2 tablespoons brandy

Vanilla ice cream or frozen yogurt

1- Combine honey, water, liqueur, and citrus zests in flambé pan over alcohol burner or in a skillet over medium-high heat. Bring to a boil, add cranberries, and simmer gently, uncovered, stirring constantly, until skins pop and sauce is slightly thickened, about 5 minutes.

2- Warm brandy in a small pan over low heat. Ignite with flame from alcohol burner or long kitchen match and pour over berries. Stir until flames die out.

3- Serve immediately spooned over vanilla ice cream or frozen yogurt.

SERVES **6**.

Note: Freeze cranberries in the bag in which they were purchased up to 1 year.

BAKED PEARS IN WINE
WITH CHOCOLATE SAUCE
○

Here, fresh, juicy pears are baked in wine and spices, then topped with a velvety smooth chocolate sauce. This is a quick-and-easy dessert to make when you are short of time.

3 firm pears, halved lengthwise and cored
½ cup dry red wine
¼ cup water
1 teaspoon sugar
1 cinnamon stick
4 whole cloves
Chocolate Sauce (page 299)
⅓ cup chopped walnuts
Fresh mint leaves, for garnish

1- Preheat oven to 350°F. Place pears, cut side down, in an 8-inch square baking dish. In a small bowl stir together wine, water, sugar, cinnamon stick, and cloves. Pour evenly over pears.

2- Bake 6 minutes, then baste generously with wine mixture and cook 3 minutes longer. Pears should be soft but not mushy. Remove from oven, let cool, cover, and refrigerate several hours.

3- Drain pears and place a pear half in each of 6 individual dessert dishes. Drizzle chocolate sauce on top. Sprinkle with nuts and garnish with mint leaves.

SERVES **6**.

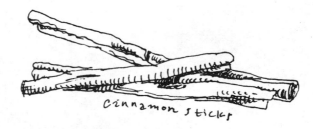

cinnamon sticks

RASPBERRIES WITH CUSTARD SAUCE

○

The pleasures of sweet-tart raspberries are countless, so enjoy them when they are in season. Here they are combined with a simple custard sauce for an elegant dessert.

CUSTARD SAUCE:

    2 cups milk

    2 tablespoons cornstarch

    ¼ cup sugar

    2 egg yolks

    1 teaspoon vanilla extract

    1 tablespoon brandy

    1 pint (2 cups) raspberries

1- To make sauce, in a heavy saucepan whisk together milk, cornstarch, sugar, and yolks. Place over medium heat and cook, whisking constantly, until mixture boils and thickens, 4 or 5 minutes. Mix in vanilla and brandy, remove from heat, and let cool slightly.

2- Divide half of the berries among 4 individual glass sherbet dishes. Divide half of the sauce among dishes. Repeat layers. Chill well before serving.

SERVES **4**.

VARIATION:

Substitute hulled strawberries for the raspberries.

BROWNIE CAKE
WITH RASPBERRY GLAZE
o

A dense, rich brownie cake crowned with a raspberry glaze and whole raspberries makes an impressive presentation.

> 2 squares (2 ounces) unsweetened chocolate,
>   broken up
> ½ cup butter, cut up
> 1 cup sugar
> ⅓ cup all-purpose flour
> ¼ teaspoon baking powder
> 2 eggs, beaten
> 1 teaspoon vanilla extract
> ½ cup coarsely chopped walnuts
> Raspberry Glaze (recipe follows)
> ¾ cup raspberries, for topping (see note)
> Fresh mint leaves, for garnish

1- Preheat oven to 350°F. In a small pan over low heat, melt chocolate with butter, stirring frequently. Let cool slightly.

2- In a bowl mix together sugar, flour, and baking powder. Stir in eggs and then chocolate mixture. Add vanilla and nuts and stir well. Pour into a generously oiled and floured 9-inch pie plate.

3- Bake until toothpick inserted in center comes out clean, about 30 minutes. Remove from oven and let cool slightly on wire rack. Run a knife around plate edges, then invert onto a cake plate. Let cool completely.

4- About 1 hour before serving, spread Raspberry Glaze on top of cake. Arrange whole raspberries on top and garnish with mint leaves.

SERVES *8* TO *10*.

VARIATION:

Omit berry glaze and raspberries. Serve warm with Chocolate Sauce (page 299) and ice cream or frozen yogurt.

Note: Berries to be used for decorating the top should be washed and drained 1 hour before using.

RASPBERRY GLAZE
○

1 pint (2 cups) raspberries

¼ cup sugar

2 tablespoons cornstarch

3 tablespoons water

1 teaspoon fresh lemon juice

1 tablespoon crème de cassis

1- In food processor or blender, purée raspberries. Place purée in fine-mesh sieve, and using a spatula, force through pulp. Discard seeds.

2- Transfer pulp to a small pan and add sugar. In a small bowl or cup stir together cornstarch and water. Stir into pan. Bring to a boil and stir until sauce is clear and slightly thickened, about 3 minutes. Remove from heat and cool slightly. Add lemon juice and crème de cassis. Cover and store at room temperature until ready to use.

MAKES ABOUT *1* CUP.

APPLE SPICE CAKE
WITH BUTTERY-RUM SAUCE
○

This cake, which keeps well, can be made one or two days ahead of serving. Top each piece with warm Buttery-Rum Sauce.

2 cups sugar

½ cup butter or margarine, at room temperature

2 eggs

2 cups all-purpose flour

1 teaspoon ground nutmeg

1 teaspoon ground cinnamon

2 teaspoons baking soda

½ teaspoon salt

1 teaspoon vanilla extract

4 Golden Delicious apples or any good baking apples, peeled, cored, and shredded (about 4 cups)

Buttery-Rum Sauce (recipe follows)

1- Preheat oven to 350°F. In a bowl and using an electric mixer, cream together sugar and butter. Beat in eggs. In another bowl or on a piece of waxed paper, stir together flour, spices, baking soda, and salt. Add dry ingredients and vanilla to butter mixture, mixing well. Using a spoon, fold in apples. Pour into an oiled 9-by-13-inch baking dish.

2- Bake until toothpick inserted in the center comes out clean, 35 to 40 minutes. Cool on wire rack. Serve warm or at room temperature with a spoonful of Buttery-Rum Sauce on top. Cover leftover cake with aluminum foil and store several days at room temperature.

SERVES *12*.

BUTTERY-RUM SAUCE
o

1 cup sugar

½ cup butter

½ cup half-and-half

1 teaspoon white rum or vanilla extract

1- In a small pan over medium heat, combine all ingredients. Stir until butter melts, sugar dissolves, and ingredients are well blended. Serve warm.

MAKES ABOUT *1* CUP.

Note: Sauce can be made several days in advance, covered, and stored in the refrigerator then reheated to serve.

GROSSMÜTTERS GINGERBREAD WITH FRESH PEARS

○

This old German gingerbread recipe is one of the best. The layer of fresh pears adds a special touch and a surprise flavor. Top with whipped cream. (What's gingerbread without whipped cream?)

> 1 cup butter or margarine, at room temperature
>
> 2 eggs
>
> ½ cup firmly packed brown sugar
>
> ½ teaspoon salt
>
> 1 cup light sour cream
>
> 1 cup dark molasses
>
> ½ cup granulated sugar
>
> 2 teaspoons ground ginger
>
> 1 teaspoon ground cinnamon
>
> ¼ teaspoon ground cloves
>
> 2 cups all-purpose flour
>
> 1 teaspoon baking soda
>
> 1 teaspoon baking powder

FRESH PEAR LAYER:

> ¼ cup butter or margarine
>
> ½ cup firmly packed brown sugar
>
> 1 teaspoon ground cinnamon
>
> 2 or 3 pears, unpeeled, cored and sliced lengthwise

1- Preheat oven to 350°F. In a bowl and using an electric mixer, cream together butter, eggs, brown sugar, and salt. In small bowl stir together sour cream and molasses. In a bowl or on a large sheet of waxed paper, mix together all remaining dry ingredients. One third at a time and beating well with a spoon after each addition, add molasses mixture alternately with dry ingredients to butter-egg mixture.

2- To make pear layer, place butter in a 9-by-13-inch baking dish and melt in oven. Stir brown sugar and cinnamon into butter. Arrange pear slices over butter-sugar mixture. Pour gingerbread batter evenly over top.

3- Bake until toothpick inserted in center comes out clean, 35 to 40 minutes. Serve warm or at room temperature.

SERVES **10**.

SEA QUEST SOUR CREAM COFFEE CAKE WITH CRUNCH SWIRL
о

Staying at Sea Quest Bed and Breakfast Inn overlooking the beautiful Oregon coast is a treat in itself, but eating a gourmet breakfast there is a treat beyond compare. This is one of their specialties.

½ cup butter, at room temperature

1 cup sugar

3 eggs

2 cups all-purpose flour

1 teaspoon baking powder

1 teaspoon baking soda

¼ teaspoon salt

1 cup sour cream

2 teaspoons vanilla extract

CRUNCH SWIRL:

1 tablespoon all-purpose flour

2 tablespoons butter, at room temperature

¾ cup firmly packed brown sugar

1 tablespoon ground cinnamon

1 cup chopped walnuts or almonds

Confectioners' sugar, for topping (optional)

1- Preheat oven to 350°F. In a bowl and using an electric mixer, cream together butter and sugar until fluffy. Add eggs, one at a time, mixing well after each addition. In another bowl or on a piece of waxed paper, mix together flour, baking powder, baking soda, and salt. One-third at a time and beating well after each, add flour mixture to butter mixture alternately with sour cream. Stir in vanilla and mix well.

2- To make swirl, in a food processor combine all ingredients. Mix briefly with several off-on pulses.

3- Pour half the batter into an oiled and floured 10-inch bundt pan. Sprinkle half the Crunch Swirl evenly over batter. Pour on remaining batter and top with remaining Crunch Swirl. Using a knife, and with a swirling motion, distribute the crunch throughout the batter. Drop pan gently on counter top to settle contents.

4- Bake until toothpick inserted in center comes out clean, 45 to 50 minutes. Let cool on wire rack for 15 to 20 minutes, then invert onto a serving plate. Dust with confectioners' sugar (if using). Serve warm or at room temperature.

MAKES ONE 10-INCH CAKE; SERVES *10* TO *12*.

VARIATION:

Add 1 cup blueberries to batter along with Crunch Swirl.

STRAWBERRIES AND CRÈME FRAÎCHE
o

Strawberries and crème fraîche served with Tea Cookies (page 294) makes a simple and luscious dessert. Crème fraîche is a French thickened cream. It can be simulated by combining sour cream with whipping cream. The result is a rich, tangy sauce that is used for dessert toppings and in sauces, soups, and baked goods. It works well in hot dishes because it does not curdle when boiled. Crème fraîche will keep in the refrigerator for about a week.

2 cups (1 pint) strawberries, hulled, sliced,
   and sugared, if desired

Crème fraîche (recipe follows)

Divide berries among 4 dessert dishes.
   Top each with a spoonful of crème fraîche.

SERVES *4*.

CRÈME FRAÎCHE
o

½ cup whipping cream
½ cup sour cream

1- In a glass container stir together whipping cream and sour cream. Cover and let stand at room temperature until thickened, 6 to 8 hours or overnight. Store in the refrigerator. Serve chilled.

MAKES ABOUT *1* CUP.

Note: Crème fraîche can be purchased in some supermarket dairy cases.

GOBLET CHEESECAKE WITH BLUEBERRY SAUCE

○

Here is a simplified version of cheesecake with the same delicious taste. Make at least a day in advance. Serve with Blueberry Sauce or fresh berries.

CRUST:

> 16 squares graham crackers, finely crushed
>
> 2 tablespoons finely chopped walnuts or hazelnuts
>
> ¼ cup butter or margarine, melted
>
> 1 teaspoon sugar
>
> ¼ teaspoon ground cinnamon

FILLING:

> 8 ounces cream cheese, at room temperature, cut up
>
> 1 cup light sour cream
>
> ¼ cup sugar
>
> 1 tablespoon fresh lemon juice
>
> Blueberry Sauce (page 300)

1- To make crust, in a skillet over high heat, toast crumbs and nuts, stirring constantly, 3 to 4 minutes. Remove from heat and add butter, sugar and cinnamon and mix well. Cool slightly, about 5 minutes.

2- Divide crumb mixture evenly among 6 goblets, pressing firmly with back of spoon onto bottom and part way up sides. Transfer to refrigerator and chill well, about 3 hours.

3- To make filling, in food processor combine all ingredients. Process until well blended. Cover and refrigerate for 30 minutes. Beat again with a spoon and then spoon on top of crumbs in goblets, being careful not to disturb crumb crust.

4- Cover and refrigerate 12 hours or overnight. Serve with Blueberry Sauce.

SERVES *6*.

VARIATION:

Serve plain with fresh fruit or chopped nuts.

COCONUT BARS ANA

○

This is an elegant little bar with a "melt-in-the-mouth" topping.

    ½ cup butter or margarine, at room temperature

    1 cup sugar

    1 whole egg and 1 egg yolk

    1½ cups all-purpose flour

    1 teaspoon baking powder

    ½ teaspoon salt

    2 tablespoons milk

    ½ teaspoon vanilla extract

COCONUT MERINGUE:

    1 egg white, beaten until foamy

    1 cup firmly packed brown sugar

    ⅔ cup flaked dried coconut

    ½ teaspoon vanilla extract

1- Preheat oven to 350°F. In a bowl and using an electric mixer, cream together butter, sugar, and whole egg and egg yolk. In another bowl or on a piece of waxed paper, mix together flour, baking powder, and salt. Add flour mixture, milk, and vanilla to butter mixture and mix well. Spread batter in an oiled 8-inch square pan or baking dish. (Batter will be thick.)

2- To make meringue, in a small bowl stir together egg white, brown sugar, coconut, and vanilla. Spread mixture evenly over batter.

3- Bake until golden on top and toothpick inserted in center comes out clean, 30 to 35 minutes. Cool on wire rack, then cut into bars to serve.

MAKES *12* BARS.

CHOCOLATE-WALNUT CLUSTERS
○

A crispy little cookie that doesn't last long at our house, especially when the grandkids come for a visit.

¼ cup butter, at room temperature

½ cup sugar

1 egg

1 teaspoon vanilla extract

½ cup plus 2 tablespoons all-purpose flour

¼ teaspoon baking powder

¼ teaspoon salt

1½ squares (1½ ounces) semisweet chocolate, melted

1½ cup chopped walnuts

1- Preheat oven to 350°F. In a bowl using an electric mixer, cream together butter and sugar. Beat in egg and vanilla. In a small bowl or on a piece of waxed paper, mix together flour, baking powder, and salt. Beat flour mixture into butter mixture. Add chocolate and stir well. Stir in nuts. Drop by teaspoonfuls, 1½ inches apart, onto greased baking sheet.

2- Bake until firm in the middle, 10 to 12 minutes. Cool on a wire rack and store in a covered container.

MAKES ABOUT **2 1/2** DOZEN.

Note: If using a non-stick baking sheet, greasing the sheet is not necessary.

SOUR CREAM FROSTIES
○

A browned butter frosting makes these cookies special for the holidays—or anytime.

½ cup butter, at room temperature

1½ cups firmly packed brown sugar

2 eggs

2⅔ cups all-purpose flour

½ teaspoon baking powder

1 teaspoon baking soda

½ teaspoon salt

1 cup sour cream

½ cup chopped walnuts

1 teaspoon vanilla extract

FROSTING:

6 tablespoons butter, at room temperature

2½ cups confectioners' sugar

Boiling water, as needed

1 teaspoon vanilla extract

1- Preheat oven to 375°F. In a large bowl and using an electric mixer, cream together butter and sugar until fluffy. Beat in eggs, one at a time. In another bowl or on a large piece of waxed paper, mix together flour, baking powder, baking soda, and salt. One third at a time and beating well after each addition, add flour mixture to butter mixture. Then stir in sour cream, nuts, and vanilla. Drop by teaspoonfuls, 1 ½ inches apart, onto greased baking sheets.

2- Bake until lightly browned, about 10 minutes. Remove to wire rack and cool completely.

3- To make frosting, in a small pan melt butter. Stir until it bubbles and turns golden brown. (The browning is important for flavor.) Add confectioners' sugar and enough boiling water to create good spreading consistency. Stir in vanilla extract.

4- Spread frosting on cooled cookies. To store, place in a baking dish in single layers. Cover with aluminum foil and store at room temperature up to 5 days.

MAKES ABOUT *4* DOZEN COOKIES.

TEA COOKIES

○

Serve this rich, crisp cookie for afternoon tea (or coffee) or with fresh fruit for a simple dessert.

½ cup butter, at room temperature

1 cup sugar, plus sugar for topping

1 egg

2 ½ cups plus 2 tablespoons all-purpose flour

1 teaspoon baking soda

½ teaspoon salt

1 teaspoon cream of tartar

½ cup vegetable oil

1 teaspoon vanilla extract

1- Preheat oven to 350°F. In a bowl and using an electric mixer, cream together butter and 1 cup sugar. Add egg and beat until fluffy. Beat in all remaining ingredients except sugar topping and mix well.

2- Form into 1-inch balls and arrange on ungreased baking sheets 2 inches apart. Place some sugar on a piece of waxed paper. Using a drinking glass, dip bottom of glass in sugar. Press each cookie flat, dipping glass in sugar before each pressing.

3- Bake until golden, 12 to 15 minutes. Remove to wire rack to cool. Store in a covered container at room temperature up to 1 week.

MAKES ABOUT *4* DOZEN COOKIES.

WINE SORBET

○

This is a refreshing sorbet to serve before the main course to cleanse the palate.

½ cup dry red wine

¾ cup ginger ale

2 tablespoons fresh lemon juice

¼ cup water

½ cup sugar

1- In a saucepan stir together all ingredients. Place over medium-high heat and stir until mixture boils and sugar dissolves. Pour into a refrigerator tray or an 8-inch square baking dish and freeze solid, about 3 hours.

2- Remove from freezer and stir thoroughly with a spoon or chop in food processor slightly. Return to tray or dish and freeze again for several hours until serving time.

SERVES *4* AS DESSERT, OR *8* BEFORE MAIN COURSE.

Note: This sorbet can also be frozen in an ice cream maker according to manufacturer's directions.

BLUEBERRY SORBET
○

Fruit sorbets retain the natural sweet flavor of fresh fruit and provide a light refreshing dessert after a heavy meal.

>   1 pint (2 cups) blueberries
>   ½ cup sugar
>   ½ cup water
>   2 tablespoons crème de cassis (optional)
>   1 tablespoon fresh lemon juice
>   1 cup ginger ale

1- In a saucepan stir together blueberries, sugar, and water. Place over medium-high heat and stir until mixture boils and sugar dissolves. Transfer to food processor or blender and purée. Strain purée into a bowl.

2- Add crème de cassis (if using), lemon juice, and ginger ale. Pour into a refrigerator tray or an 8-inch square baking dish and freeze solid, about 3 hours.

3- Remove from freezer and stir thoroughly with a spoon or chop in food processor slightly. Return to tray or dish and freeze again for several hours until serving time.

SERVES **4**.

Note: This sorbet can also be frozen in an ice cream maker according to manufacturer's directions.

CHEESE AND FRUIT TRAY
o

An assortment of apples, grapes, and cheeses attractively arranged on a tray is just the right ending for a heavy meal. Serve with crackers and a glass of good-quality port.

1 large Rome Beauty apple or other crisp red apple

1 large Granny Smith apple or other crisp green apple

Juice of 1 lemon

1 cup water

5 to 6 ounces Monterey Jack cheese

5 to 6 ounces Brie cheese

4 ounces blue cheese

1 bunch seedless red grapes

1 bunch seedless green grapes

Assorted crackers

1- Cut unpeeled apples in half and then cut lengthwise into slices ¼ inch thick. Cut off core area from each slice and discard. (Edge will be straight.) To keep apple slices from turning brown, place in a bowl with lemon juice and water and turn slices to coat evenly. Let stand 5 minutes, then drain and arrange slices, alternating red and green, in a semicircle at one side of a large tray.

2- Arrange cheeses in center of tray and place grapes alongside one side of cheeses. Lay crackers in a row on opposite side of tray. Serve with a small knife for slicing cheese. May be made ahead, covered, and refrigerated up to several hours. Serve at room temperature.

SERVES *10* TO *12*.

FOURTH OF JULY ICE CREAM

○

*This summertime tradition is a treat anytime of the year. Serve with
fresh fruit or sauce of your choice (recipes follow).*

2 cups milk

1 cup sugar

4 eggs, beaten

2 cups half-and-half

1 tablespoon vanilla extract

1- In a saucepan stir together milk, sugar, and eggs. Place over
medium heat and cook, stirring constantly, until mixture thickens slightly and coats the back of a spoon, about 5 minutes. Remove
from heat. Cover and chill well, about 2 hours.

2- Stir in half-and-half and vanilla. Pour into ice cream maker and
freeze according to manufacturer's directions.

MAKES ABOUT *1 1/2* QUARTS; SERVES *8*.

VARIATION:

Fresh Peach Ice Cream. Add 4 peaches, peeled (see note, page 269),
pitted, and chopped to the mixture before freezing.

BUTTERSCOTCH SAUCE
○

Allow this sauce to cool completely before serving.

⅔ cup sugar

¼ teaspoon baking powder

5 tablespoons butter

⅓ cup buttermilk

2 teaspoons light corn syrup

1 teaspoon vanilla extract

1- In a small saucepan stir together all ingredients. Bring to a boil and boil, stirring frequently, until slightly thickened, about 5 minutes. Cool completely.

MAKES ABOUT *3/4* CUP.

CHOCOLATE SAUCE
○

This sauce uses cocoa, which has less fat than baking chocolate. It will not get hard when cold, so it can be kept, covered, in the refrigerator for days. It is delicious served hot or cold.

¼ cup unsweetened cocoa powder

1 tablespoon cornstarch

½ cup sugar

1 cup hot water

1 tablespoon light corn syrup

1 tablespoon butter

½ teaspoon vanilla extract

1- In a small saucepan stir together cocoa, cornstarch, and sugar. Slowly stir in hot water and then add corn syrup. Bring to a boil and cook, stirring constantly, until slightly thickened, about 2 minutes. Remove from heat and stir in butter and vanilla.

MAKES ABOUT *1* CUP.

BLUEBERRY SAUCE
○

Serve this sauce at room temperature or chilled.

  3 tablespoons sugar
  ½ cup water
  1 tablespoon cornstarch
  1 tablespoon fresh lemon juice
  1 pint (2 cups) blueberries

1- In a saucepan combine all ingredients except blueberries. Whisk until blended, then add blueberries. Bring to a boil, stirring constantly, and boil until juice is clear and sauce is slightly thickened, about 2 minutes. Cool, then transfer to a bowl, cover, and store in refrigerator. Serve cold or at room temperature.

MAKES ABOUT *2* CUPS.

TOFFEE TOPPING
○

A good spur-of-the-moment dessert sauce. This sauce is wonderful served warm or at room temperature on vanilla ice cream or frozen yogurt. Top with a sprinkling of nuts.

  1 cup firmly packed brown sugar
  1 cup strong brewed coffee
  ½ teaspoon vanilla extract
  2 tablespoons brandy

1- In a small pan over low heat, stir together brown sugar and coffee. Simmer, uncovered, until slightly thickened, about 10 minutes. Remove from heat and stir in vanilla and brandy. Serve warm or cool.

MAKES ABOUT *2* CUPS.

FROZEN PEACH-APRICOT AND BRANDY SAUCE

o

A delightful sauce that freezes well up to 1 year and may be refrozen. Make it when the peaches are ripe and keep it on hand in the freezer for spooning over vanilla ice cream or pound cake.

2 cups sugar

4 cups fresh orange juice

Juice of 1 lemon

¼ cup apricot brandy or brandy

4 large ripe peaches, peeled, pitted, and sliced
   (see note, page 269)

5 or 6 apricots, peeled, pitted and sliced
   (see note, page 269)

Apricot brandy or brandy

1- In a saucepan over medium heat, combine sugar, orange juice, lemon juice, and brandy. Cook, stirring, until sugar dissolves. Add peaches and apricots and stir to mix well. Remove from heat, let cool slightly, and then freeze in quart containers.

2- Remove sauce from freezer 1 hour before serving; mixture should be icy when served. Stir sauce, then spoon desired amount over ice cream. Top each serving with 1 tablespoon brandy.

MAKES ABOUT *2* QUARTS.

INDEX

○

TABLE OF EQUIVALENTS

○

*The exact equivalents in the following tables
have been rounded for convenience.*

US/UK

oz = ounce
lb = pound
in = inch
ft = foot
tbl = tablespoon
fl oz = fluid ounce
qt = quart

METRIC

g = gram
kg = kilogram
mm = millimeter
cm = centimeter
ml = milliliter
l = liter

LENGTH MEASURES

⅛ in ....3 mm
¼ in ....6 mm
½ in ....12 mm
1 in ....2.5 cm
2 in ....5 cm
3 in ....7.5 cm
4 in ....10 cm
5 in ....13 cm
6 in ....15 cm
7 in ....18 cm
8 in ....20 cm
9 in ....23 cm
10 in ....25 cm
11 in ....28 cm
12/1 ft ....30 cm

LIQUIDS

US	METRIC	UK
2 tbl	30 ml	1 fl oz
¼ cup	60 ml	2 fl oz
⅓ cup	80 ml	3 fl oz
½ cup	125 ml	4 fl oz
⅔ cup	160 ml	5 fl oz
¾ cup	180 ml	6 fl oz
1 cup	250 ml	8 fl oz
1½ cups	375 ml	12 fl oz
2 cups	500 ml	16 fl oz
4 cups/1 qt	1 l	32 fl oz

WEIGHTS

US/UK	METRIC
1 oz	30 g
2 oz	60 g
3 oz	90 g
4 oz (¼ lb)	125 g
5 oz (⅓ lb)	155 g
6 oz	185 g
7 oz	220 g
8 oz (½ lb)	250 g
10 oz	315 g
12 oz (¾ lb)	375 g
14 oz	440 g
16 oz (1 lb)	500 g

OVEN TEMPERATURES

FAHRENHEIT	CELSIUS	GAS
250	120	½
275	140	1
300	150	2
325	160	3
350	180	4
375	190	5
400	200	6
425	220	7
450	230	8
475	240	9
500	260	10